CREATIVE IDEAS FOR
SMALL GARDENS

CREATIVE IDEAS FOR
SMALL
GARDENS

Anthony Paul

HarperCollins*Publishers*

First published in 1994 by
HarperCollins Publishers
Reprinted 1994

Created exclusively for HarperCollins by
Anthony Paul, **Steven Wooster** and **Susan Berry**
Unit 30, Ransome's Dock, 35 Parkgate Road
London SW11 4NP
Tel: 071 228 4332

Designed by **Steven Wooster**
Copyright © **Anthony Paul** 1994

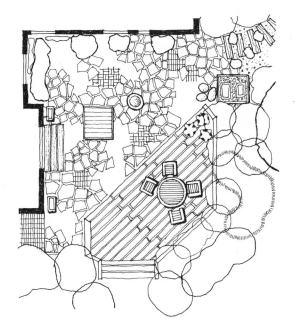

For HarperCollins Publishers
Commissioning Editor **Polly Powell**
Project Editor **Barbara Dixon**
Jacket Design **Caroline Hill**

A catalogue record for this book is available from the British Library

ISBN 0 00 412905 9

Colour reproduction in Singapore, by Colourscan
Printed and bound in Italy, by Arnoldo Mondadori Editore
Distributed in the United States by HarperCollins Publishers,
10 East 53rd Street, New York, NY 10022

Contents

Ferns galore
OPPOSITE The limited space afforded by a narrow alleyway is planted with maximum impact using all the available surfaces. Even the walls play host to an interesting collection of ferns, including the maidenhair fern (*Adiantum pedatum*) and *Nephrolepis* sp.

Bizarre beauty
RIGHT A pair of baroque-style chairs carved from tree trunks crosses the borderline between furniture and sculpture.

Green river
BELOW In an unusually emphatic planting statement, a river of mondo grass (*Ophiopogon japonicus*) flows down this steeply sloping small garden, echoing the shape of the boulders but softening the form.

MUCH OF THE FUN of gardening is in the planning, and armchair gardening has now become a serious hobby. But gardening is not all sitting around and watching the grass grow under your feet, although it is a good way of relieving stress in a world that is becoming increasingly pressurized. It is not a particularly expensive hobby and, in most cases, a well-planned garden is an investment. It is certainly an investment in your environment, as you may develop a garden that pro-

vides you with a place for reflection and inspiration, or a place that integrates outdoor living with the interior of your home.

A garden is also an organic, cyclical journey as plants develop, mature and inevitably die. To watch the seed of an idea grow, from the planning stage into a mature garden, is one of the most satisfying and rewarding aspects of designing a garden. Success comes slowly and an ideal solution may take much planning, and revision, to achieve but it is better, and cheaper, to translate these ideas on to graph paper first.

Elements of planning

Perhaps the starting point in the planning has to be the limitations of the site. Your garden will naturally impose certain restrictions on what you are able to do. While some of these restrictions can be overcome artificially, in general it is much better to 'go with the flow' and adapt your ideas to suit the site. If your garden is naturally shady, then look for plants that enjoy those conditions; if it is damp and waterlogged, make a virtue of it and grow lots of lush, large-leaved moisture-loving plants.

Climate is another vital factor since it affects not only the choice of plants, but how you use the garden, and the kind of materials employed. Fierce sun can be just as damaging and as difficult to deal with as strong winds and frosts. You need to have a good look around the garden, and see if there are areas that are well-protected – a warm, sunny wall, perhaps, or a screened area that gets a lot of sun – so that you can grow some more interesting, half-hardy or tender plants.

If you do not have much in the way of rainfall, consider carefully how much time you will have to water your garden. If it is limited, consider installing an automatic drip-watering system; the layout for this may also help to determine what you plant and where you do so.

Work out which way your garden faces, because the aspect again will determine the choice of plants. Do not fall into the trap of thinking that a south-facing spot is necessarily always the warmest. An east-facing garden will warm up quickly in the early part of the year, when daylight hours are shorter. West-facing areas receive the lingering warmth of a summer sunset, and are perfect for evening entertainment and for dinner parties al fresco.

Soil is rarely, if ever, perfect. You do need to examine it carefully to find out where its shortcomings lie. A pH analysis testing (you can buy kits to test it, which are quick and easy to use) will indicate the level of acidity and alkalinity, and help you to decide

Big is beautiful
RIGHT Many people think
that small gardens need
small plants. The
opposite is often true.
Even massive plants like
this *Gunnera manicata*
are not out of place in
small town gardens, and
through their sheer mass
deceive the onlooker into
believing the garden is
much larger than it really
is. The ferns in the foreground are *Matteuccia
struthiopteris*.

Atmospheric effects
BELOW Lighting plays a
significant part in altering
the atmosphere in the
garden. This table setting
– elegant and sophisti-
cated by day – turns into
a mysterious environment
at night, when subtly lit
by candles and spotlights.

on the right plants, as some plants, such as rhododendrons and azaleas for example, will not grow in
alkaline soil. Owners of brand-new properties often
find that there is little, if any, topsoil, in which case
there is no option but to import it – an expensive
business. It is possible to improve soil that is too
heavy or too light by adding plenty of organic matter,
and if you want to keep the plants in your garden in
good condition, maintaining the organic content of
the soil properly is an important factor.

Although you are pretty well stuck with the size
and shape of the plot you have, there are certain
tricks you can employ to change the apparent shape
of the plot. A small or uninteresting 'long' narrow
strip of a garden can have its proportions disguised
by screens of foliage and flowers that mask its true
length and help it to appear wider than it is. A garden that is boringly square and squat may benefit
from being compartmentalized so that you cannot
take it all in at a glance.

Usually when I design a garden for a client I start by drawing up a list of priorities, or the types of feature that are wanted for the garden, and any major practical items that are needed, such as a greenhouse, a small pool or even a compost heap. The next consideration is to know who will be using the garden and for what purpose. Children or pets must be taken into account, as must the safety of the former in planning any water features, or in the choice of plants – my favourite giant hogweed (*Heracleum mantegazzianum*) has poisonous sap, for example. Will the owners want to spend time relaxing in the garden, and if so, in what manner? Should there be a patio area close to the house for al fresco entertaining, for example, and if so, how can the site be improved for this purpose. Is privacy required, and is the site overlooked by other houses? The other very important question is the time available to spend in the garden. There is no point in designing a wonderful tapestry of plants for people who are not

Linking feature
LEFT Conservatories can play a major role in linking the house to the garden. The fact that you are half-way between garden and the house allows the planting and furnishing style to mingle effortlessly. The bold architectural style of this conservatory requires a similarly forceful colour scheme in the planting, provided here by pots of pelargoniums. The use of one colour – blue – for the window frames and roof supports has been matched by using a single predominant flower colour in the planting.

11

in the slightest bit interested in gardening, nor is it sensible to include plants whose flowering season starts just at the point when the owners of the garden take off on holiday.

Finding a suitable style

Taste is always a much-disputed topic, and I, for one, would certainly not insist that my taste in gardens or in plants should be the same as everyone else's. There are, nonetheless, certain principles inherent in good design, and these should underpin any style choices.

The first is to ensure that the elements you are planning to include in the garden are suitable for the purpose, and fit together as a coherent whole. If in doubt, opt for less rather than more and go for one big item, rather than several small ones. Be ruthless about throwing anything out, moving it or digging it up if it does not fit the overall scheme. There is very little place for sentiment in good design, but there is equally nothing to stop you building an attractive garden around one single, worthwhile inherited feature, such as a particularly handsome tree or shrub. In fact, most good garden design needs a clear starting point from which the plan can develop.

One of the advantages of employing a garden designer, apart from their experience at the job, is the fact that they draw out of their clients exactly what their tastes and interests are by asking specific questions. To design your own garden successfully, it pays to ask yourself the same kind of questions. What styles of garden do you admire? What elements in the garden most appeal to you? What kind of plants do you prefer?

On a more personal level, I cannot sufficiently stress the importance of using handsome foliage plants and water in any garden design. One quick look through this book will probably make that clear enough! But architectural plants add structure, solidity and form to the design, while water creates a marvellous change of pace. If you crave colour in a small garden, add it in containers of annuals and bulbs, which can be changed seasonally against the more permanent backdrop of the foliage planting.

Once you have created a good framework for the garden, the secret is to relax your grip and allow the plants to self-seed to some extent. Nothing looks worse than a garden which shows too clearly the hand of man. Success lies in getting a good balance between organized planning and nature's own contribution to the garden.

Tastes in gardens change periodically, but the best gardens are those that reflect most accurately their owner's interests and preferences. Rather than slavishly copying any particular design, try to take the best ideas and adapt them to your own needs. I hope this book provides you with both inspiration and some practical advice.

Eau de vie

LEFT If it is at all possible to include water in a garden design, then I do. The wildlife, the reflective qualities, the sound and the sheer joy that it brings to any garden gives another dimension to life. Water plants are among the most interesting and exciting plants for a small garden, and the strong lush shapes and bright colours are some of the most rewarding in the plantsman's repertoire.

One of the simplest ways to understand how to construct a garden from scratch is to follow in the footsteps of a professional garden designer, as they go through the process of design from plan to completion. Five small gardens, each with a very distinctive look, are included in this chapter, with detailed descriptions of their design and construction, together with plans.

Planning

◆ ITALIANATE CITY GARDEN ◆
◆ COUNTRY WATER GARDEN ◆
◆ SHADY TOWN GARDEN ◆
◆ CONTAINER GARDEN ◆ ORIENTAL GARDEN ◆

Italianate city garden

Statuesque columns and a trompe l'oeil doorway create an air of romantic fantasy in this tiny London garden, sandwiched between tall buildings. Frost-tender plants grow in the sheltered micro-climate.

THIS WAS A real peach of a garden to work on. It had been left to its own devices for about 20 years, but it had several excellent features: good high brick walls on three sides, several levels, and – the *pièce de résistance* – an unusually large, ancient fig tree at the end of the garden. One of the branches of this fig was almost horizontal, supported on old chunks of wood. In addition to the fig tree, there was a splendid wisteria which must have been planted at the turn of the century. It climbed, anaconda-like, over the house, and filled the garden with heady scent in early summer.

These plants formed the centrepiece of the design, and the first consideration was to find some more visually pleasing way to support the fig's branches. Three old concrete columns were painted with a distressed, Italianate finish, and proved ideal. The paving in the garden was York stone, and after lifting, cleaning and relaying, it was returned to its original glory.

For the patio directly in front of the living room, warm slate with flashes of terracotta running through it, laid in a diagonal pattern, made the area look broader than it was. The space was used for containers of clipped and shaped shrubs and trees, laid in a small avenue, to take you down the steps into the main area of the garden.

As the garden faced south, and was sheltered by high walls, we experimented with some tender plants, such as a sago palm (*Cycas revoluta*), a group of *Clivia miniata* and a lemon tree in a pot. Simple, double rimmed, Italian pots were chosen as a theme throughout the garden. The York stone in this part of the garden was relaid with larger than average gaps, and grouted with a mixture of 50:50 sharp sand and soil, into which small plants of *Alchemilla mollis*, *Erigeron karvinskianus*, *Viola labradorica* 'Purpurea' and *Soleirolia soleirolii* were planted. These quickly took hold, and turned the area into a floral carpet.

The columns supporting the fig needed something sculptural and interesting at their base, and here I put *Zantedeschia aethiopica*, the arum lily, with *Actinidia chinensis* to scramble up the columns themselves.

On stage
RIGHT The view into the garden from the living room was designed to emulate a theatre set, as if some Shakespearean actor would step out from the bushes. Although the garden is in the heart of London, it has an unusually private and intimate atmosphere. With the doors open from the living room, you are directed straight to the heart of the garden under the columns supporting the ancient fig tree, and past the topiary avenue.

Because the garden was less than 15m (50ft) in length, some feature was needed for the back wall to expand the boundaries. A door was painted, half ajar, with a view of an Italian scene, with a church, glimpsed through it. The door was surrounded by a trellis arch, which was planted with the scrambling *Cobaea scandens*, the cup and saucer plant. In just one year, it covered most of the trellis and the back wall. The trellis itself was painted a muddy blue-green, to blend in with the planting.

For the shady area leading down to the basement, I used the tree ferns that I loved so much as a boy in New Zealand. They are wonderful plants to have in any garden that is frost-free, but are difficult to obtain and quite expensive. I planted only one specimen, *Dicksonia fibrosa*, in a pot and added a small group of native New Zealand ferns, *Asplenium bulbiferum*, to surround it. *Clivia miniata*, in pots, was added to this planting scheme, along with that other shade-lover, *Aspidistra elatior*. Its long broad leaves are an excellent foil for ferns or trailing plants. I also took a gamble on *Spar-mannia*, which is

Special feature

ABOVE The garden in spring has one predominant feature – a 75-year-old wisteria which climbs up the house and around the overhanging balconies. To bring it into view from the living room, I designed a small metal arch to support it so that the full benefit of the cascading mauve flowers could be appreciated.

A Original fig tree
B Columns
C Water feature
D Steps to basement
E Chairs and table
F *Trompe l'oeil* door
G York paving
H Arch with wisteria

Protected environment

RIGHT The garden is so warm and sheltered, thanks to its protective high walls, that even sub-tropical plants stay out all year round and thrive. The *Canna indica* flowers in late summer. The houselime (*Sparmannia* sp.) next to it is covered with thick bubble plastic in the winter.

normally grown as a house plant in Britain, but has so far survived the winter for four and a half years. It is pruned hard back in winter but comes back each summer, producing its handsome soft green leaves and attractive white sails.

Choosing the rest of the plants for the garden was sheer delight. *Ensete ventricosum*, a very tough Japanese banana plant, was used as a feature against the back wall, along with *Tetrapanax papyrifera*, the rice-paper plant. Both have wonderfully architectural foliage. A group of *Ligularia* 'The Rocket' was planted under the shade cast by the fig tree.

Plant for all seasons
LEFT *Clivia miniata* is a South African lily normally grown in temperate climates as a houseplant but in this garden it flowers out-of-doors from early April until June. It is tucked into a warm corner for the winter and left unwatered in these months. After flowering, it still makes a lovely foliage plant.

Shady selection
BELOW At the base of the fig tree, I planted a collection of shade-loving plants, including *Ligularia* 'The Rocket', various geraniums, *Fatsia japonica* and ferns. Behind the fig, a large-leaved *Tetrapanax papyrifera* provides a sheltering canopy over the end of the garden. Busy Lizzies are planted with ferns into an old concrete urn, paint-finished in terracotta. Candles are positioned liberally for night-time atmosphere.

1 *Musa* sp.
2 *Acer palmatum* in pot
3 Tree fern (*Dicksonia fibrosa*) in pot
4 *Choisya ternata*
5 *Clivia miniata* in pots
6 *Cycas revoluta* in pot
7 *Pittosporum tobira* in pot
8 Clipped box (*Buxus sempervirens*) in pots
9 *Canna indica* in pots
10 *Sparmannia africana*
11 Underplanting ferns – *Asplenium bulbiferum*
12 Mixed ferns – *Asplenium, Dicksonia* and *Polystichum*
13 *Soleirolia soleirolii* in paving
14 *Hosta sieboldiana*
15 *Trachycarpus fortunei* in pots
16 *Aspidistra elatior* in pots
17 Busy Lizzies in pot
18 *Ligularia* 'The Rocket'
19 *Geranium sylvaticum*
20 *Tetrapanax papyrifera*
21 Tree fern (*Dicksonia antarctica*) in pot
22 *Zantedeschia aethiopica*

Country water garden

The plan in practice

RIGHT This view of the garden, taken from above, illustrates its simple shape and the emphasis given to the cider press water feature, with a small path that leads from this sitting area to a small decked portion (out of view). Water flows from the cider press into the two bog gardens either side of the central path, which are planted with hostas, ligularias, primulas, and lythrums.

Strong contrasts

BELOW Planted in the bog garden next to the cider press is a drift of *Primula florindae* mixed with *Mimulus lutea*. The scent from this tall primula fills the air in the evenings. The deep purple of the *Lythrum salicaria* makes a strong contrast.

In this 20 by 10m (65 by 32ft) garden, the slight change in level and the curving path disappearing through planting create a greater illusion of space; an effective treatment for a relatively small area.

ONE GOOD FEATURE can be all that is needed as a peg on which to hang an original garden design. I had a client whose hobby was collecting architectural relics and garden statuary. Among the objects he had purchased was a huge old stone cider press, which was shaped like a millstone, with a rill running all around to let the cider drain off to the vat below. It made a wonderful central water feature for the area he asked me to design outside the kitchen, where, as luck would have it, there was a disused well.

The water feature and bog gardens

A shallow dished pond, filled with river-washed pebbles, was constructed around the well, the millstone manoeuvred into position to cap the well, and two vents created in the pond to allow surplus water to drain away into two bog gardens on either side of the path leading up to the well. A small submersible pump was fitted into the well, and the water was then pumped up through a bamboo spout which poured over the stone of the press, around the rill

Continuous flow
RIGHT The old cider press is built above a well, allowing water to pump up through a bamboo spout and circulate through the rill of the press back to the well. Any splashed water, or rain water, flows out over the pebbles through the gap in the brick surround to feed the bog garden. *Miscanthus sacchariflorus*, the giant grass behind, provides a background screen.

On the right tracks
BELOW The railway sleeper path was designed to look like an old railway line. *Sagina subulata* and wild strawberries (*Fragaria vesca*) grow in the beach gravel between the sleepers. In the foreground, on the left, is *Cynara cardunculus*. On the right is *Primula florindae*. The yellow flowers at the back are those of *Ligularia* 'The Rocket'.

and into the pond. As the pond area was so shallow, it was also safe for children.

The kitchen floor of the house was tiled in terracotta Provençal brick, and the same tiling, which was also weatherproof, was used for the seating area outside the kitchen. This was shaped as a large circle to reflect the shape of the cider press and around the outer part a low maintenance gravel garden was created, in which herbs, such as thymes, sages and chives, were planted.

On either side of the path leading up to the water feature two semi-circular bog gardens were dug and lined with plastic (punctured in places to allow some drainage) so that the soil in these gardens would remain moist. For a continuous display from early spring to late summer, early-flowering marsh marigolds (*Caltha palustris*), primulas, Japanese irises (*I. ensata*), hostas, mimulas, and *Lythrum salicaria* were planted in large groups.

Paths and planting

Between the seating area and the path to the cider press, a wedge of sleepers was cut to make a fan arrangement, set at the same level as the paving bricks, with a sleeper edge inserted between the paving bricks and the bog garden. A little gravel path was constructed around the back of the bog garden, also lined with railway sleepers.

A garden that has a strong, geometric plan, as this one does, needs a similarly emphatic planting scheme. In this garden, the plants were chosen not simply for their shapes and forms, but to make large clumps that would also suppress weeds. Hostas are very good subjects for this purpose: *Hosta crispula*, which enjoys moist soil, and *H. fortunei*, with its soft lilac-coloured flowers, both make an impact.

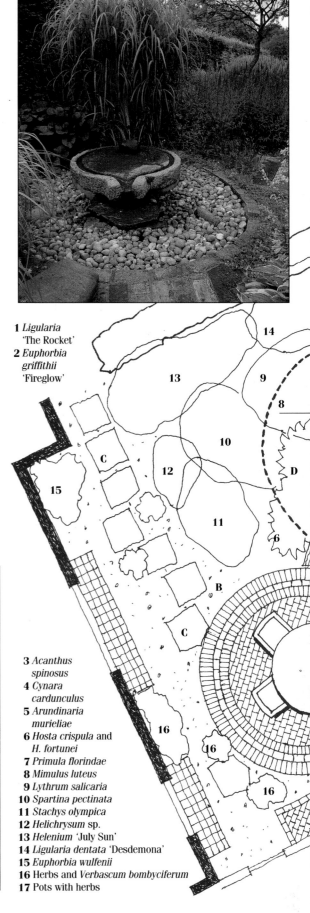

1 *Ligularia* 'The Rocket'
2 *Euphorbia griffithii* 'Fireglow'
3 *Acanthus spinosus*
4 *Cynara cardunculus*
5 *Arundinaria murieliae*
6 *Hosta crispula* and *H. fortunei*
7 *Primula florindae*
8 *Mimulus luteus*
9 *Lythrum salicaria*
10 *Spartina pectinata*
11 *Stachys olympica*
12 *Helichrysum* sp.
13 *Helenium* 'July Sun'
14 *Ligularia dentata* 'Desdemona'
15 *Euphorbia wulfenii*
16 Herbs and *Verbascum bombyciferum*
17 Pots with herbs

When planting up a garden with a preponderance of perennials, it is also imporant not to neglect spring-flowering plants, and fritillaries, pulmonarias, violas and hellebores are all worth incorporating to prevent the garden looking naked earlier in the year. Be sure to repeat the groups of plants around the garden, to give continuity and to draw the eye from one part of the garden to the next.

31 *Rudbeckia* 'Herbstsonne'
32 *Thalictrum flavum*
33 *Rosa rubrifolia*
34 *Lonicera* sp.
35 *Macleaya cordata*
36 *Coreopsis verticillata*

A Sleeper decking
B Gravel
C Stepping stones
D Bog gardens
E Cider press
F Sleeper path
G Sleeper steps
H Gravel path

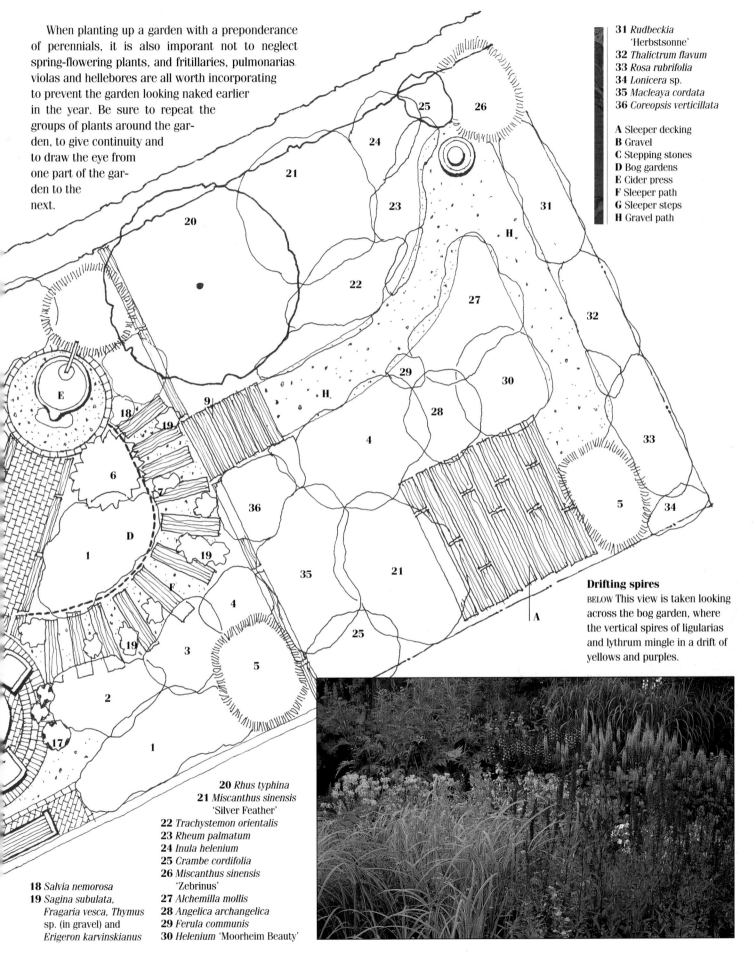

Drifting spires
BELOW This view is taken looking across the bog garden, where the vertical spires of ligularias and lythrum mingle in a drift of yellows and purples.

18 *Salvia nemorosa*
19 *Sagina subulata, Fragaria vesca, Thymus* sp. (in gravel) and *Erigeron karvinskianus*
20 *Rhus typhina*
21 *Miscanthus sinensis* 'Silver Feather'
22 *Trachystemon orientalis*
23 *Rheum palmatum*
24 *Inula helenium*
25 *Crambe cordifolia*
26 *Miscanthus sinensis* 'Zebrinus'
27 *Alchemilla mollis*
28 *Angelica archangelica*
29 *Ferula communis*
30 *Helenium* 'Moorheim Beauty'

Shady town garden

This plan of a 12 by 8m (38 by 26ft) garden shows how limited space can be overcome by combining a few natural materials such as timber, stone and gravel with dramatic planting to create a stylish modern garden.

THERE IS NO garden that does not require some maintenance, even though it may just be tidying up the hard surfaces or clearing the leaves from a patio or deck. (Very few people would not vacuum-clean the inside of the house, so there is no reason why this small outside space should not receive the same degree of attention.)

The clients, who own an elegant town house, gave me the brief that the garden should be an extension of the house, as though it had just crept forward by another few yards. The garden itself was small – only 12m by 8m (38ft by 26ft) – and was overshadowed by a large terrace of houses at the rear whose upper windows looked right over the garden. The sunlight that did manage to penetrate the garden was obstructed by a huge sycamore in the neighbour's garden to the west.

Owing to the low light level, my first thought was that a light-coloured material was needed for the seating area and the fencing, which would help

Layout and design
RIGHT & BELOW The two views of this garden demonstrate the simplicity of the construction and planting. The design centres around a stepped deck, stained grey, with a sitting area under a pergola, planted with *Actinidia chinensis*, at the back of the garden. Although the garden is quite shady, the light-coloured deck helps to reflect light back onto the plants. Two spots are positioned under the pergola, shining back to the table, so that even on a dull day this outdoor room looks cheerful. Ferns, hostas, Japanese maples and *Aucuba japonica* provide rich, textural, foliage colour and contrast.

24

Screened from view
BELOW The surrounding walls are constructed from interwoven reed panels, which were made into timber screens, about 2m (6ft) tall, to enclose the entire garden. The cheap but effective fencing can last for at least 10 years.

Sweetly scented
BOTTOM *Pittosporum tobira* is in flower, filling the garden with the scent of orange blossom. This plant is in a pot, and is surprisingly hardy if it is given a sheltered spot.

reflect light back into the space. The garden was approached directly from the kitchen through a set of huge double doors which afforded a good view of the whole of the small space. For the surface in front of them, I chose a simple wooden deck pattern, stained a light grey to keep the light effect I wanted, but stepped back to give the illusion of a deeper garden. The larger deck was to serve as a seating space, but it also concealed a trapdoor for a sandpit for the clients' small son. To give privacy at the rear and to increase the feeling of seclusion, a pergola was constructed to form a small open roof for plants to climb over.

One of the most important considerations in deck construction is to consider the pattern it will create when finished. The lines of the deck can be used to take the eye across the width to broaden the garden, or to give the illusion of space. A 45° angle of timber lines will serve this end and I like to contrast this angle with a

contrasting one where the deck, perhaps, changes level. This idea worked very well for this small garden which had two smaller decks stepped down from the main sitting space.

The walls presented a problem as they were all different. One was a fence, another a broken-down brick wall and another a trellis of some sort. Again pale-coloured material was needed to reflect light, and so panels of interwoven reeds (which are sturdy and last up to 10 years outside) were used. These are best built into a frame with a bracing cross-

A Table and chairs
B Decking
C Pergola
D Pot with annuals, on stand

1 *Pittosporum tobira* in pot
2 *Hosta sieboldiana* 'Elegans' in pot
3 *Dryopteris filix-mas*
4 *Hedera deltoides*
5 *Aucuba japonica*
6 *Hedera sagittifolia*
7 *Actinidia chinensis*
8 Yuccas in pots
9 *Fatsia japonica* 'Variegata'
10 *Lonicera* 'Late Dutch'
11 *Arundinaria murieliae*
12 *Hosta sieboldiana* 'Elegans'
13 *Acer palmatum dissectum* 'Atropurpureum'
14 *Trachelospermum jasminoides*
15 *Cordyline australis*

Fruit and foliage
LEFT Light filters through the pergola, clothed with *Actinidia chinensis*. Although it seldom fruits in a temperate climate, the kiwi fruit plant is well worth growing for its lovely strong leaf form, and its ability to grow quickly to cover arches and pergolas.

member to make them able to withstand winds. These panels come in 2m by 2m (6ft by 6ft) sizes and are quick and inexpensive to put up.

Planting ideas

The planting for this garden was crucial, not only in respect of the low-maintenance considerations, but to create a strong visual element from the kitchen window. I decided not to go for any fussy plants but instead to opt for plants that would quickly grow to produce the architectural style that would suit the clients' wishes. To emphasize this point, I chose yuccas and bamboos as the major

features but set these off with a filigree of light leaves and ferns and a prize specimen *Acer palmatum dissectum* 'Atropurpureum' as a foil for the light grey of the deck, as well as some variegated foliage plants such as *Fatsia japonica* 'Variegata' and *Aucuba japonica*, to cheer up the garden in the winter months. Of course, some of my favourite plants, such as *Ligularia dentata* 'Desdemona', were included along with *Hosta sieboldiana* which quickly established itself and made a good feature plant next to the Japanese maple. *Trachelospermum jasminoides* and honeysuckles (*Lonicera* sp.) were chosen for the screens on the fences, but this planting was kept to a minimum to allow the light colour of the panels to stay soft and reflective.

Container garden

In this 12 by 9m (38 by 30ft) garden, living space has been maximized, and it has been decorated with brightly painted furniture and groups of flower-filled terracotta pots, surrounded by sheltering hedges.

WHEN ASKED by many people, 'What is your favourite small garden?', I very often refer to this garden. Not because I designed it – it is in fact the work of a Belgian interior designer, Walda Pairon – but because I like the clear simple approach that she has adopted. The alluring feature of this carefully thought-through design is its stage-set approach, by which I mean its changing elements in the form of pots, furniture and ornaments.

Surface areas

The garden's principal feature is its surface material and the way it has been laid. The surface is an old Flemish paving brick, which is long and thin in shape, that was used for roads or canal paths. These old bricks are about a hundred years old, and are fairly easy to obtain in Holland or Belguim, but similar materials in the form of granite or brick setts are available in other countries. The beauty of these old bricks lies not only in their warm and slightly chipped surface but also in their colour, a sort of mauvy-grey. The elongated shape of the brick allows it to be set in tight rows, following a simple interlinking pattern, and it is laid in sharp sand – the traditional way of laying this particular material.

To help generate a feeling of space Walda Pairon has laid the bricks on a 45 degree angle across the garden, drawing the eye along the lines to each boundary hedge. Here and there in the hard surface pattern she has created gaps for planting shrubs.

Hedges as boundaries

The real joy of this garden is in its soft hedging boundaries. These act like a stage backdrop giving a feeling of enclosure and privacy, while the surface provides a platform for the actors – in this case clipped topiary trees, summer sub-tropical plants such as citrus, agapanthus, bougainvillea and hydrangeas – to perform. The more tender of these plants are reared through the winter in what the continentals call a winter garden, and what we would call a greenhouse or conservatory, and then brought out to flourish in summer. Each year these pots get put back into different positions, creating a different look.

Orchestrated colour
RIGHT This intimate area is brought alive by the colourful furniture and unusual pot shapes and ornaments dotted around. The paving is old Flemish brick. Clipped bay trees, citrus, hostas and hydrangeas in pots form the planting focus.

Laurus nobilis. All can be purchased in mature form from specialist nurseries, which may have already clipped them into some interesting shapes.

This garden makes no attempt to mimic or copy a traditional country garden, but announces quite clearly that it is an extension of its designer owner's living area. It provides a very intimate space where people can sit outside in privacy and enjoy their leisure pursuits of eating or relaxing in a small, almost secret, garden.

Tender delights

ABOVE The charm of this garden lies in the way the plants are grouped among tables and ornaments. The lemon tree (*Citrus* sp.) is overwintered in a greenhouse but the *Agapanthus* in the foreground, which are not in flower, can be left in a sheltered position, provided they do not freeze in winter.

Furniture and ornaments

In its furniture and ornaments, this garden is very special. The colour speaks for itself, zinging and shape-enhancing, with a glowing property which I love, because it is set off so well against the green foliage and grey surface, like an artist's canvas. A painted bench against the back hedge cleverly draws the eye to the rear part of the garden, while two round tables, made from wrought iron and slate, fit well with the style. Walda Pairon is a fine garden stylist and knows how to mix colour and form in her garden. The terracotta frogs and other ornaments get changed regularly, and the addition of one or two well-shaped unplanted pots adds special interest.

The garden requires very little maintenance and could be easily reproduced for a small country or town garden, although hedges take a while to become established. Nowadays, it is possible, at a price, to purchase clipped plants in pots and also to obtain quite mature hedging which will require only one or two years to establish. Good evergreen plants to use for formal pots are *Ligustrum japonicum*, *Buxus sempervirens*, *Viburnum tinus* and

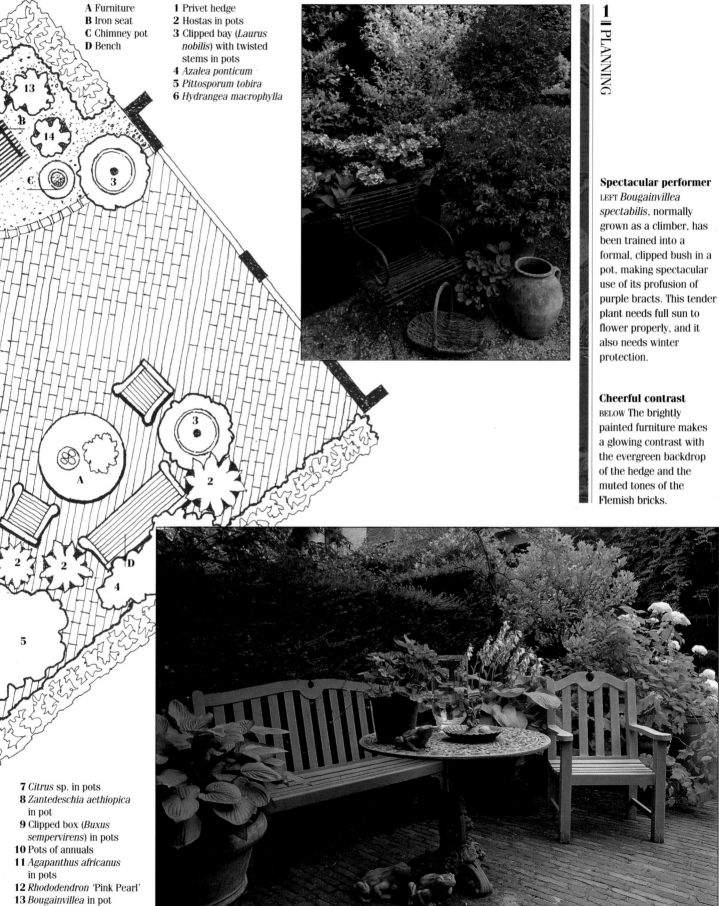

A Furniture
B Iron seat
C Chimney pot
D Bench

1 Privet hedge
2 Hostas in pots
3 Clipped bay (*Laurus nobilis*) with twisted stems in pots
4 *Azalea ponticum*
5 *Pittosporum tobira*
6 *Hydrangea macrophylla*

7 *Citrus* sp. in pots
8 *Zantedeschia aethiopica* in pot
9 Clipped box (*Buxus sempervirens*) in pots
10 Pots of annuals
11 *Agapanthus africanus* in pots
12 *Rhododendron* 'Pink Pearl'
13 *Bougainvillea* in pot
14 Strawberry plants in pots

Spectacular performer
LEFT *Bougainvillea spectabilis*, normally grown as a climber, has been trained into a formal, clipped bush in a pot, making spectacular use of its profusion of purple bracts. This tender plant needs full sun to flower properly, and it also needs winter protection.

Cheerful contrast
BELOW The brightly painted furniture makes a glowing contrast with the evergreen backdrop of the hedge and the muted tones of the Flemish bricks.

Oriental garden

The natural elements of water, stone and rock have provided a successful solution to this 15 by 7m (48 by 23ft) low-maintenance garden. The reflecting properties of the water enhance the sense of light and space.

ONE OF THE most enjoyable aspects of garden design is that no two gardens are ever the same to design. For this garden, the client was my own twin brother. The brief was to design an oriental garden that was not necessarily Japanese. My brother travelled very often to the Far East, and had acquired a collection of oriental *objets d'art* and garden pots from Thailand and Indonesia.

The garden itself measures a mere 15 by 7m (48 by 23ft), but it had the benefit of four mature fruit trees, one of which was a particularly beautiful old apple tree. The existing trees and plants were transcribed on to the paper plan, and then a large area of water was drawn into the centre of the garden, crossed centrally to divide the garden into two separate spaces. One of these – at the rear of the garden – allowed enough room for a generous sitting area, where my brother could dine al fresco.

Surface materials

Blocks of granite, kerbing stones and old York stone flags, found in an architectural salvage yard, formed the basis of the hard surfaces. The corner kerb stones were a particularly lucky find as, turned flat

The layout and design
RIGHT & OPPOSITE The overall view of the garden from the house shows the directional flow of the old granite road kerbing, taking you across the pond to the sitting area beyond. The sound of splashing water is heard from both the central fountain, which helps to aerate the water in the pond, and the bamboo spout, from the sitting area, which pumps water up from the pond over a granite basin. Bamboos, ferns and mossy plants soften the hard surface and help to create the garden's oriental flavour.

and overlapped, they provided a splendid oriental bridge over the pool. The other kerb stones were used to edge a path leading back to the conservatory door, and two slabs of granite were turned into steps. Between the kerbs of the path, river pebbles formed a softer surface into which mosses, ferns and baby's tears (*Soleirolia soleirolii*) were planted. On the other side of the bridge, rounder stepping stones were used to continue the path up to the seating area, which was paved with the York stone

slabs, laid far enough apart for mosses, small mat-forming perennials and creeping thymes to be planted between the stones.

The water feature
The pond itself was constructed using a butyl liner, over which stones of about 4cm (1½in) diameter were positioned to mask the edges, and to act as a mulch under the planting. To create some movement in the water, and to remain in keeping with the

Unusual bridge
RIGHT The bridge over the pond was constructed from two old granite road kerbs set flat, instead of on their edges, on top of one block of granite in the water.

Deceptive planting
BELOW The soleirolia seems to grow into the water, but this is, in fact, duckweed (*Lemna minor*), an invasive aquatic plant. The gently sloping edges of the pond allow wildlife to visit it to drink. The granite stepping stones have been set in gravel to make a natural-looking surround.

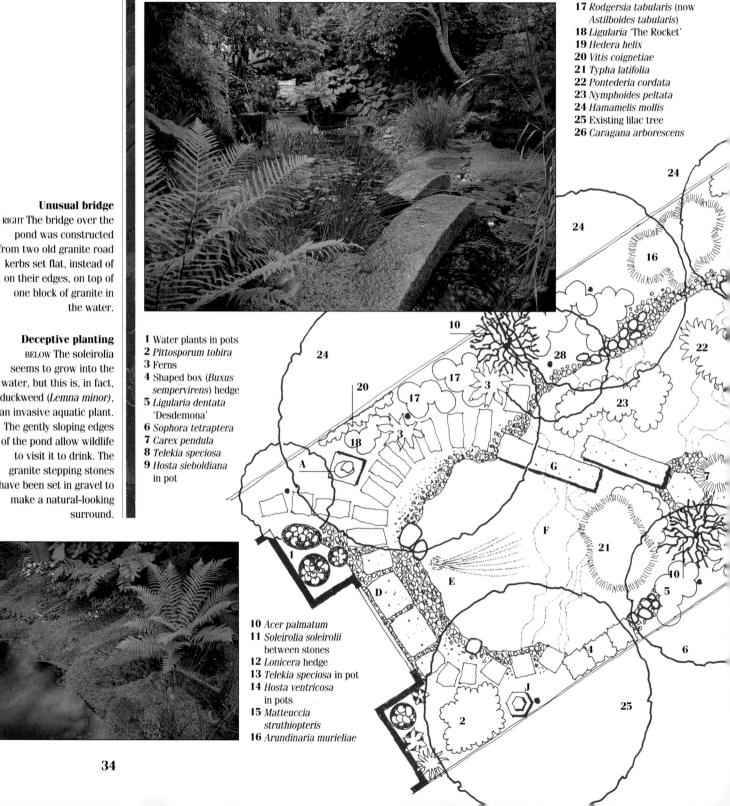

17 *Rodgersia tabularis* (now *Astilboides tabularis*)
18 *Ligularia* 'The Rocket'
19 *Hedera helix*
20 *Vitis coignetiae*
21 *Typha latifolia*
22 *Pontederia cordata*
23 *Nymphoides peltata*
24 *Hamamelis mollis*
25 Existing lilac tree
26 *Caragana arborescens*

1 Water plants in pots
2 *Pittosporum tobira*
3 Ferns
4 Shaped box (*Buxus sempervirens*) hedge
5 *Ligularia dentata* 'Desdemona'
6 *Sophora tetraptera*
7 *Carex pendula*
8 *Telekia speciosa*
9 *Hosta sieboldiana* in pot

10 *Acer palmatum*
11 *Soleirolia soleirolii* between stones
12 *Lonicera* hedge
13 *Telekia speciosa* in pot
14 *Hosta ventricosa* in pots
15 *Matteuccia struthiopteris*
16 *Arundinaria murieliae*

oriental theme, I used two large wedges of granite to make a central water feature. A sculptor friend carved a hemisphere in the top wedge to serve as a water bowl, and trimmed the stones so that they fitted neatly on top of each other.

On the top part of the wedge, I used a bamboo spout through which a copper pipe was threaded, and which took water from the small submersible pump in the pool over the top of the bowl, creating an attractive tinkling sound.

Elements of planting

The next job was the planting, which was probably the most fun of all. Firstly, my brother's large Indonesian and Thai pots were placed in strategic positions, and for each pot either a Japanese maple (*Acer palmatum*) was chosen or it was filled with water to grow water-loving plants.

The pond edges were planted with *Scirpus* grasses, a fine reed, and a large group of *Pontederia cordata* in the water's margins. *Typha latifolia*, the tall reedmace, was planted closer to the house to give some feeling of height in this part of the garden. At the base of the reedmace, I planted a small water lily as a skirt around the reeds. To the west side of the garden, sheltered by the reed screen wall, *Rodgersia* (now *Astilboides*) *tabularis* created just the right oriental look, with its large dinner-plate shaped leaves. Behind the rodgersias we planted a strong group of bamboos (*Arundinaria murieliae*) which, with their feathery leaves and soft arching habit, make a great display in winter. My brother is particularly fond of witchhazel – for what obscure reason I do not know – and so three good plants of *Hamamelis mollis* were planted in the corners of the garden, offering early flowers and scent at a time of year when very little else is happening in the garden.

The garden has had the added bonus of providing a real haven for wildlife, and birds daily come to drink from the pond, or feed from the bird table that my brother placed in one of the apple trees. Some years ago, the pond was filled with tadpoles from my own lake, and the garden now teems with frogs, which breed happily.

A Sculpture
B Japanese waterbowl and
    spout
C Stone beach
D Steps in granite concrete
E Water jet
F Pond
G Bridge
H Table and benches
J Japanese lantern

Handsome giant
BELOW This amazing example of *Hosta sieboldiana* 'Elegans' in a pot – its foliage nearly 1.5m (5ft) across – almost dwarfs the chair next to it. York paving looks best if grouted with gravel, in which plants can grow and self-seed, as they have here.

One of the really exciting and 'fun' elements of gardening is to design and build a garden in an area where the available space presents a definite challenge. Many places, such as roofs, basements and side alleys, suffer from lack of good soil, or insufficient light or too much exposure to the elements. This is where the fun and the challenge comes in. There are problems to be solved, concepts to be thought through and ideas that are going to have to be practical as well as fantastical.

Linking spaces

Architectural links

The importance of the link between house and garden should never be ignored when designing small gardens, since the architecture is a particularly prominent backdrop.

THE STRUCTURE OF ANY well designed small garden is almost as important as the structure of the house to which it belongs. Plants themselves become a living link between the two entities, fusing the garden and house together. Although the idea of roses around the door of a country cottage is hardly new, if the smell of wisteria or jasmine has ever wafted in on a summer day through your bedroom window, you will understand how wonderful it is to have scented plants growing against your house.

Situation is all-important in forming a link, and this also determines the way you should approach the subject. Modern house builders and architects today, with a few exceptions, seem unaware of the way that their buildings sit in the landscape, and how links can be created to make a house blend seamlessly with its surroundings

The drama and excitement of a small garden can depend on the success of the marriage between the

Clipped circles
RIGHT The curved architectural detailing of the house is reflected in the sweeping circles of brick, gravel and box – an unusual variation on the traditional geometry of a formal parterre. Although the planting has been kept predominantly green, the subtle variations are highlighted by the clever clipped forms and shapes.

Framed view
OPPOSITE The use of this rose pergola which appears to connect with the house but, in fact, focusses the eye on the garden, rather like an inverted telescope, was an idea I had to fuse this Swiss garden and house together. I also tried to create a ground pattern that would offer some extra perspective when viewed from the inside.

Minimalism rules
BELOW This garden makes
a seamless extension to
the house itself, divided
only by a long, winding,
water rill that follows the
lines of the architecture
of the building it flanks,
and actually forms part of
the internal architecture.

style of the garden and that of the house. For example, clipped evergreen box, privet and pittosporum are ideal subjects to wrap around a turn-of-the-century villa-style house. Not only do they enhance the vernacular architecture, but they create a look which seems comfortable and appropriate to the overall style. Neatly clipped hedges, trees in pots, and maybe even a small parterre, could continue this theme into the rest of the garden.

In any small garden, most of it is in view from the house at all times, which means that special care has to be taken with the design and siting of any special features. Framing a view of the garden from a window is an intrinsic part of the success of its design, since you are going to spend quite a lot of time indoors looking out upon it. Make sure that the

expensive piece of sculpture you bought is sited in the best position for viewing from inside as well as outside, and think about the view of the garden at night. Lighting can play a wonderfully successful role in linking house and garden together at night (see page 168).

Linking surfaces

An important factor when creating linking devices is to understand the surface materials and techniques that are at your disposal. Although the surface materials used in a garden are not always the same as those used inside the house, in many cases you can create a feeling of continuity between these materials by taking paving stones or tiles inside the house or out in the garden to create some sort of flow, so that there is no harsh, obvious, cut-off point where house ends and garden begins.

This idea works particularly well if you have a conservatory or kitchen leading into the garden which can then perhaps be tiled in the same material as the patio, or, conversely, the hard stone floor of the patio can be echoed in similar stone floors indoors. Bricks, for example, could be used as an edging device, and then repeated in steps or paths leading away from the house.

I make no secret of my enthusiasm for timber decking, which makes the perfect linking material between house and garden. Decking can be painted in the same colours as those used on the house itself, such as for window-frames or doors. Timber bridges and walkways, or verandahs, can be constructed which lead from the house to the garden to create a series of levels that add a real design feature to the garden.

Walls, fences and screens

The choice of walling (if you are building from scratch) or what you choose to do with existing walls is another important element in how well the garden and house fit together in small spaces. If the materials are very different, and do not look good together, then consider ways of disguising the walling or fencing using climbing plants or possible screens of reed or bamboo (see pages 118-25). Make sure any new low walls are constructed in sympathetic materials – repeating either the colour or texture of the house walls perhaps – and that the proportions are in scale.

Water features

Water is one of the nicest ways of bringing the house and garden together. A water feature set against the house wall, pouring into the garden, is one such link. A New Zealand architect I know has actually designed a house and garden so that the water comes into the house itself, with large stepping stones taking you from the house out into the

patio, which appears to be an island, surrounded by water which flows back into the house. Although this is not something that could be copied in cold climates there are other means of achieving the same end. Peter Aldington, an English architect, has designed his house with a pool that actually laps against the house wall itself, separated from the living area only by a huge plate-glass window, that makes it appear as if the pool is part of the house.

Pergolas and covered walks

Sometimes, if the house and garden do not sit very comfortably together, walkways or pergolas can be constructed which help to bridge the gap by bringing the planting close to the house itself. They can also be very practical as well, providing a covered walk between a garage, for example, and the house. Any walkways need to be surfaced with material that is both attractive and sensible. Make sure that any paths and steps are wide enough for safety, and light them if necessary at night.

Softening effects

The hard edges of both house and garden architecture frequently need some form of softening effect. Plants in boxes or tubs on window ledges, balconies, or small flat roofs, are an excellent device for adding a feeling of warmth and intimacy to an otherwise cool exterior. Where doors and windows can be opened to allow access to the garden, lush arrangements of foliage plants in the vicinity will encourage a feeling of continuity between house and garden.

Linked by water

BELOW The low off-white walls and dark gravel of the garden (and the carpet of dark purple foliage in the picture, opposite) echo precisely the strong definitions produced by the walls and windows of the house behind. Garden and house seem inseparable, as balconies protrude into the garden, and water invades the internal space.

Entrances and front gardens

Simple statements work best for entrances and front gardens. Try to adhere to the three principles of garden design – unity, utility and proportion – and keep the colour palette limited – perhaps to two or three colours.

THE MORAL SAYS we should not judge a book by its cover, but all too often we do, and a house is frequently judged by its entrance. It is an area on which too little time is spent, and needs a carefully thought-out statement.

Humphry Repton, one of the great English garden designers in the 18th century, made the point that gardens should have unity, utility and proportion. This means that the design should have a consistent theme, that it should be fit for the purpose and that its various elements should be in scale with each other. These points are particularly relevant to any entrance. Even if you only have a few feet in front of your house, it is well worth while giving that space proper attention.

Front paths
Almost every entrance has a path of some description leading to the front door. Surfaces are discussed in detail on pages 108-129 but it is important to emphasize here that the choice of materials for a path in such a prominent position must be appropriate. Make sure you pick one that blends well with the architectural style of the house, and which is also durable and practical. Even very narrow strips of soil either side of a front path can be put to good use for plants. Low formal planting in the form of a ribbon of clipped evergreen shrubs on either side of the path always works well. Clipped box, lavender or santolina are excellent for this purpose. Alternatively, you could create a small avenue of standards of fuchsias, honeysuckle or roses, underplanted with a softening cloud of catmint (*Nepeta* sp.) or unclipped lavender.

Mix and match
BELOW & OPPOSITE Planting can echo the contrasting colours of the entrance and the scheme can harmonize with them, in the same way that you would choose fabrics and furnishing for a room. Soft mounds of aromatic plants, such as English and French lavender, in purple and mauves, pick up the colour scheme of the intricately detailed Colonial-style verandah.

Planting schemes

It is far better in a very small space to concentrate on one or two allied groups of plants, perhaps hebes and santolina, or rosemary and lavender, than to indulge in a complicated planting scheme. Over-designed, these small spaces can look contrived and very busy. Opt instead for emphasis, with the odd accent plant in a pot or a carefully positioned piece of sculpture. It is worth making use of any front fences as a support for climbing plants, provided they can be neatly trained and properly maintained. Unity will be achieved by planting in groups, rather than choosing too many different varieties, as will limiting the colour scheme to one or two colours. Do not neglect the house walls as an area for growing interesting plants. The large-leaved ornamental vine, *Aristolochia durior* (syn. *A. macrophylla*), is a very good plant for a front wall, as its handsome foliage creates almost sculptural shapes.

If you do not want to spend much time on the front garden, then use an interesting surface material and position some large, well-chosen containers at strategic points rather than simply create a large expanse of dull hard surfacing with nothing to

Colour co-ordinated

LEFT The fence and gate of this Colonial-style house have been designed to echo the wooden construction of the house itself, and to pick up the design detailing. Low clipped hedges on either side of the path add to the symmetry; the terracotta tiles echo the colour tones of the roof, and cleverly lead the perspective to the front door of the house.

relieve the monotony. Alternatively, pick a few shrubs with good foliage that will give a year-long display of interesting leaf colours and shapes.

Steps

Many front gardens have a step, or steps, up to the front door and, provided they are wide enough, they are the ideal place for matching pairs of containers. If there is enough room, use pots that are large enough to look imposing, and plant them up with something really eye-catching. You can opt either to change the scheme in the pots with the seasons, picking a display of tulips, all in one colour, for spring, followed by perhaps lilies or nicotianas, and then chrysanthemums in autumn, or you can go for something more permanent and sculptural – clipped topiary shapes in box or yew, for example. Containers of brightly coloured geraniums or busy Lizzies on a flight of steps, one for each step, make a superb display for an otherwise dull feature.

If you do not have the money to buy matching pots, then paint those you have the same colour. Rather larger front gardens, with a depth of more than a few feet, can have more elaborate planting schemes, but on the whole ambitious flower borders are best avoided in a front garden.

Containers

I do not think I have ever designed a garden without making use of containers for plants. They are one of the garden designer's best tools, because they enable you to move the plants about at will. The flexibility they give you is invaluable, but the container itself needs to be considered as part of the overall design, and you also need to be careful how you position them. There are two principal points to bear in mind. Firstly, plan your containers as an entity; do not just rush off and buy any pot that takes your fancy – think first whether it will create a unified scheme with those you already have.

Elegant and Edwardian
OPPOSITE The mauves, golds and browns of the antique tiles used for the front path are echoed in the colours of the planting scheme, in the form of the mop-headed hydrangea on the right, with starry blue heads of *Agapanthus* sp. and the golden foliage of *Robinia pseudoacacia* 'Frisia'.

Oriental feel
BELOW The bamboo and timber gate house, roofed with hand-made tiles, creates an authentic oriental atmosphere for this little courtyard.

Secondly, make sure the plant material and the container set one another off. If in doubt, always opt for a single large pot (for larger plants) or a group of the same pots in a smaller size. Mixed pots and containers do not work nearly so well, and small pots reduce the impact. It is far better to go for a large container planted with one, or at the most, two different plants. Terracotta pots from the Mediterranean region have been popular for a long time, and their classic shapes seem to fit in with almost any style of garden. In addition, there is now a good range of glazed and unglazed pots available from China and the Far East, and they are usually reasonably good value. Colours such as dark blue, sepia, green or Indian red work well in most colour schemes. Wood, stone, clay and metal are the best materials for containers, the choice depending on the style of the garden.

Colour schemes

The colour in the front garden is not necessarily limited to the plants. Some of the most successful designs for front gardens marry the colour scheme of the gate and front fence to the paintwork of the

Spiky contrast

RIGHT A bold architectural statement requires a similarly bold planting scheme if the planting is not to be overwhelmed by the buildings. Here, the sharp outlines of a group of large *Agave* sp., with its spiny, glaucous, blue-green foliage, makes a powerful contrast of shape and colour with the flat expanse of the plain painted walls of the modern building behind.

Pairs of pots

OPPOSITE, TOP Clipped balls of box (*Buxus* sp.) in square stone tubs add a touch of symmetry and formality to this sophisticated front entrance, the rounded shapes of the box making an attractive contrast with the vertical lines of the architecture.

Vertical emphasis

OPPOSITE, BELOW This entrance relies on two columnar trees in pots to give more emphasis to the door itself, while the softer mounds of planting – such as *Erigeron karvinskianus*, artemisia, rosemary and lavender – have been used to relax the severity of the surrounding architecture, the colour of the paint-work echoing that of the mounds of foliage.

house behind. One such solution is to use a second paint colour to pick out the architraves to the front door and windows, and to repeat this colour for the gate and fences. A planting scheme which tones or contrasts can turn an architecturally dull front entrance into something singularly eye-catching, with relatively little outlay. The same idea can be copied for window boxes or planters, but be careful not to overdo the mix-and-match effect or it will all start to look too contrived. Ideally, any colour coordination should look accidental and effortless rather than too deliberate.

Basements and shady spaces

Although awkward spaces to design, given the lack of light, there is plenty of scope to use your imagination to give these areas a real lift, with trompe l'oeil *paintings on the walls, perhaps, or by careful positioning of a stunning piece of sculpture.*

A VERY SMALL dark plot, perhaps only a few feet square, in the heart of a city, appears at first glance to be a gardener's nightmare. But such sites are often quite easy to transfrom if you look at them from a different point of view. You have to garden by illusion, first of all by creating a sense of space and volume, and then emphasizing the mood you have in mind. Shady small gardens are often some of the loveliest, and there are many wonderful plants that prefer part- or full shade. The most taxing situations for planting can be overcome by looking closely at what grows in nature: for basements, opt for plants that grow in the dark places under trees – such as ivies or ferns.

The walls and fences can be painted in white or pale colours that will catch or hold the light; on the other hand, deep blues, greens or deep ochres can be used to absorb light and add depth and mystery to an already dark area. Attention to detail is always important in enclosing these spaces and in a small garden this is of primary importance to the ultimate design. It is a question of framing up the garden, of bringing the whole together before you consider what you are going to do on the ground. My passion for the ferns which do so well in these shady gardens stems from the tree ferns (*Dicksonia antarctica*) that I loved so much when I was growing up in New Zealand. Their soft fronds, which roll up like curled asparagus tips, denote to me one of the most primitive of plants. Indeed, tree ferns themselves will grow well in pots in frost-free pockets, protected from full sun, and make wonderful structural shapes. There are also many other types of fern you can use, and these are invaluable for creating a natural look in any shady space. Large evergreen plants are not too common in temperate climates so those with handsome foliage, such as *Fatsia japonica* or *Aucuba japonica*, are to be cherished. They work well as single specimens in pots, but are also fine plants for an area where they have to survive on neglect. They like to be under-watered rather than the reverse, and will thrive in very low light.

Introducing colour

Shady spaces are often the result of buildings or trees removing most, if not all, of the direct sunlight. Here it is important to provide colour not only by painting the walls, but also by adding bright colourful pots, ceramic objects or beautifully painted flower pots or boxes. It is also possible to use brightly coloured materials on the surface, perhaps decking painted or stained in one of the many colours now available. Blue, deep red and even dark grccns can look good. I once designed a blue-decked garden and painted the furniture in strong apple-green. Do not be afraid to make bold contrasts, because often such an idea, which may seem a bit bizarre, can be the stroke of genius that holds the whole garden together.

Shady city gardens often lack an abundance of flowers, but there are one or two old favourites,

A touch of white
OPPOSITE Shady areas, like this area alongside the wall of a house, need reflected light to bring them to life. Marguerites (*Chrysanthemum frutescens*) in pots bring light and life to the space.

Tiny basement
BELOW An impossibly small dark basement has been vastly improved by painting the walls white, adding a white trellis above, and planting with bold, architectural dracaenas and ferns.

such as busy Lizzies (*Impatiens* sp.), which will stay in flower almost all summer, and can be overwintered in cold climates in greenhouses. Spring bulbs come into flower before trees come into leaf, and for brightening up a shady garden, bulbs in pots are invaluable. I love tulips, particularly the white 'Triumphator' tulip, but *Fritillaria imperialis*, which comes in yellows, oranges and reds, is one of the most handsome and striking specimen bulbs for a medium-sized container.

Succulent colours in tulips – particularly apricots and pale pinks – and the 'Parrot' tulips with their multicoloured petals look marvellous if well positioned in large groups around a feature, or grouped together on a shelf. The bulbs can later be replaced by hostas, ferns, ligularias or bergenias.

Containers and pots

Pots are an essential ingredient for a shady basement type garden as they allow you the flexibility to

move the plant into a position with more light if needed. Outside the back garden of my own house in Surrey, I have three large Scots pine trees which cast a continual shadow over the terrace. I garden in this way, interchanging pots, making new arrangements every summer, and planting up bulbs in my pot collection, and acquiring every year a new plant that will provide a different theme to the garden.

Sculptural pieces, such as stone or wood carvings, can be positioned on small plinths or tables so as to offer some relief from the monotony of having all pots or features sitting at one height. There may be room to build something like this as a permanent feature where a shelf or a large plinth around the ample girth of the tree acts as a display area for these objects or for plants which can be attractively arranged. Many small and dark basement spaces can be used for small visual displays, perhaps viewed from the kitchen or framed through a window from an inside room. The art here is to choose, perhaps, a single feature such as a small water fountain or a very good piece of art which can be carefully lit at night (see page 168). The addition of a few plants in containers to soften the edges is probably all that is needed. In many cases, the simplest statements work the best.

Supporting role

LEFT Basements and small town gardens often present a problem of access. Here, the wrought-iron spiral staircase is not only an interesting feature in its own right, it provides a support for the planting. Many good foliage plants, such as ivies, hostas and ferns, do well in shade.

Formal symmetry

LEFT This geometrically designed courtyard is appealing in its simplicity. Good design points are the neat plinths of clipped box surrounding the bases of the trees (*Robinia pseudoacacia*), and the way in which the diagonal lines of the stone paving add to the width, and break up the perspective.

Alleys and passageways

Narrow, dark areas between buildings or alongside garden walls demand a special approach if they are to be planted successfully. It pays to try to alter the dimensions visually to increase the width and to choose plants that flourish in shade.

SOME OF THE MOST successful garden designs take advantage of space that might well be considered unplantable. The long dark passageway that links the front garden to the back is one such example. Another is the narrow alley that extends down the side of a town house.

Altering the dimensions

To widen a long narrow space, the planting should break across it at intervals. Straight ribbon-like planting will appear to increase the length; mounds of rounded or sprawling plants at intervals along its length will help reduce it. A focal point at the end of the path will help to foreshorten the perspective. Certain colours recede and others advance. If you want to bring the end of the alleyway closer, red flowers at the far end will reduce the distance; blue, on the other hand, will increase it.

Large-leaved foliage plants also help to break up the space (especially if you contrast different plant forms and leaf shapes), as do contrasts of texture – glossy next to felted leaves, and large, simple leaves next to finely divided, feathery ones.

As with any small space, try to unify and simplify the theme of the design to prevent it looking bitty: repeat groups of plants along the length of the alleyway or keep to a single colour theme.

Singing the blues
LEFT A change in contour in a long passageway alongside a house has been turned into a feature by painting the simple wooden steps a really zingy shade of blue. The flowerheads of *Agapanthus* and the foliage of the carpeting plants alongside – *Ajuga reptans* and *Cerastium tomentosum* – echo the blue tones, as does that of the large shrub, *Abelia grandiflora*.

Contrasts of form
OPPOSITE This long narrow area has been made to appear wider by using interesting contrasts of leaf colour, shape and texture punctuated with pieces of sculpture to draw the eye away from the confines of the plot. By concentrating on a simple green and white colour scheme, the flower interest kept to a long ribbon of dazzling white petunias and a pot or two of busy Lizzies, the area gains unity as well.

Touch of spice

RIGHT In this narrow
alleyway running along-
side a New Zealand town
house, the soft divided
leaves of native ferns and
plants in pots and bas-
kets make a good con-
trast of both colour and
texture against the white
walls of the house, and
the plain terracotta tiles
of the pathway, whose
rich colour helps to bring
warmth to an otherwise
cool colour scheme.

Shady spaces

OPPOSITE Alleys are fre-
quently in shade for at
least part of the day, and
in this walk-through
garden I designed in
Switzerland a small deck
was installed by a water
feature to allow a quiet
sitting space surrounded
by soft shade-loving
perennials with good leaf
interest, in the form of a
group of mixed hostas,
Iris sibirica, *Miscanthus
sinensis* and *Ligularia*
'The Rocket'.

Planting solutions

In one London garden I know, a narrow, very shady
alleyway running alongside a garage has been
turned into an attractive formal area, with ivies covering the walls and fences, and ribbons of ferns
planted along the base of the walls, with old quarry
tiles forming a central path leading to a small statue
on a niche in the end wall, also framed in ivy.
Despite limited variety in the planting, this small
area has a unified design and works extremely well,
providing an interesting contrast of pace to the
design of the rest of the garden, which is full of sun-
loving herbaceous perennials. The element of surprise is one of its strengths.

If the area is extremely shady, you are limited in
your choice of plants, but one solution is to have
containers of plants that you replace periodically, so
that the low light levels do not adversely affect the
planting. Those plants that do flower in shade tend
to have white or pale flowers, and to me look most
natural in shady areas of the garden, while adding a
luminosity to the planting scheme. Green and white
colour schemes are restful and elegant. A large container filled with arum lilies, *Zantedeschia aethiopica*, or my favourite white 'Triumphator' tulips,
would look very good on a narrow table set against
one of the walls. So, too, would pots of the large-
leaved hosta, *Hosta sieboldiana* 'Elegans' with its
elegant waxy, deeply veined, blue-grey leaves. Ferns
are also good subjects as they will fit successfully
into narrow, shady spaces, making an interesting
textural ribbon at the base of a wall.

Roof gardens

The main priority with roof gardens is to find ways of creating shade and shelter, not only to shield the garden and its occupants from wind and weather, but to give a much-needed feeling of privacy.

THE AUTHORS OF gardening books sometimes patronize their readers as far as the subjects they choose to discuss are concerned. If I am guilty of that here, it is because I have learned, from experience, that you cannot be too careful with roof gardens. Perhaps the first and foremost consideration for any roof garden must be its access. Does it have a convenient method of getting onto the roof through a reasonable door or roof light that opens? There is no point in trying to build a roof garden where you have to squeeze through a narrow or awkwardly placed window to get on to it.

Weight

If access presents no problems, then the next criteria is weight. Is the roof you intend to use strong enough to support heavy plants and boxes? You can easily check this with a building surveyor, who can gauge how much your roof design is likely to weigh and recommend ways around the problem if the weight loading is insufficient. In roof gardens I have designed, I have spanned the roof with a complete set of stronger beams and built decks on top to support flower boxes which have been placed around the perimeter where the weight is best supported.

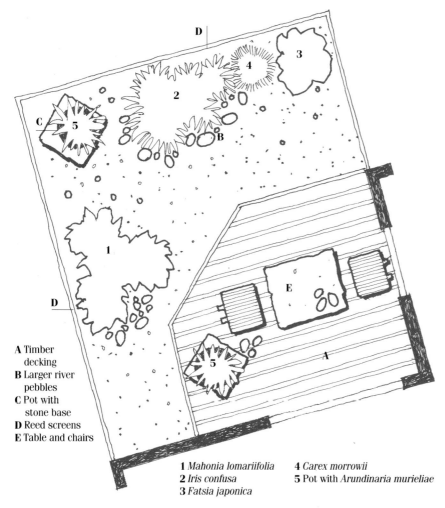

A Timber
  decking
B Larger river
  pebbles
C Pot with
  stone base
D Reed screens
E Table and chairs

1 *Mahonia lomariifolia*   4 *Carex morrowii*
2 *Iris confusa*   5 Pot with *Arundinaria murieliae*
3 *Fatsia japonica*

Decking is one of the best ways to surface a roof garden. If your design is to be more formal, then lightweight ceramic tiles are the next best solution.

Safety and protection

The other essential elements to consider are safety and protection. As a result of their elevated situation, many roof gardens will suffer from wind and exposure, unless you create some form of protection. Without it, the roof is not an environment for happy plants, and certainly not one for happy humans. Shelter can present a problem where views are a principal attraction, and here you have to be inventive. Trellis screens are nearly always the best solution; they break up the wind by letting it pass through them, they do not obscure the light, and they still permit the view to be appreciated if portholes are left in the trellis. Glass screens are excellent for protection around sitting areas, for example, but they are expensive. Where there is a need to hide an unattractive view, and a solid screen is required, reeds, bamboos or even brush or heather are first class materials. Make sure the fixings for all screens are strong and well located (see page 126). The safety factor for children is important. Screens should be high enough to prevent children climbing

Oriental roof garden

LEFT This tiny roof garden was the extension of an oriental-style interior, and I designed the furniture, deck and planting to reflect this concept. Bamboos have been planted in Chinese pots, raised on timber or stone plinths. *Iris confusa*, a dry-loving but quite tough iris, with an almost bamboo-like quality to the leaves, has been planted into a mound of soil laid directly on to a membrane to hide the original roof surface. A layer of gravel was used as a mulch, which can also be walked on. The table is simply a slab of York stone set on two cedar wood bearers, and the Japanese chair was designed to be in style. The use of alternating widths of timber for the decking helps to give the surface contrast, and the reed screens add an oriental touch while providing useful shelter and some privacy.

Intimate spaces
RIGHT & BELOW This small roof garden has been given protection from wind, and also some privacy, with timber trellis that is approximately 3m (10ft) high. Trellis is ideal for this kind of situation as it also provides a support for the planting. Painting or staining it an interesting, but subdued, colour will also improve its appearance.

over them and strong enough to prevent an adult from falling through them.

Proper drainage from the roof is essential to ensure that no water seeps through to the ceilings below. Again a building surveyor can help you, but if you are confident that the roof is already waterproof, then be careful not to puncture any asphalt or other waterproof seal when laying wooden decking or other materials. Also ensure that you do not affect the drainage with the new material.

Pots and planting
A cosy, well-protected, warm area for sitting on a roof garden is invaluable and here you may well be able to build in some furniture against a wall or into

to withstand dry conditions. Many of the sub-shrubs, like cistus, euphorbias, senecios, lavenders, genistas, cytisus, santolinas, hebes, felicias, dorinicums and osteospermums, are all excellent plants for roofs, with good flowering over a long period, and with tough leathery leaves. Some have the ability to trail over container edges, making lovely flowing shapes.

Often plants which relish standing sentry-duty against strong winds are the same plants that survive near the seaside. Plants such as tamarix, elaeagnus and griselinia are excellent subjects for this type of screen, and serve to protect more delicate plants behind them, acting as pioneers.

Lighting

Lighting on a roof garden is one of the most important features, and being able to use the roof at night, particularly when you live in the city, is a very important asset. Be careful not to have lights which are positioned so that they dazzle or blind you, or shine into neighbours' windows. Downlighters are probably the best, with a few uplighters shining up into feature plants. See also pages 168-73.

Tough customers
ABOVE When planting a roof garden you need to choose plants that will cope with exposure. Nothing comes much tougher than cacti, which enjoy some sunlight and fresh air in summer. Plants in pots always gain in impact from being grouped together.

a corner. Around it you can position plants in containers that add to the protection. If you use timber containers, make sure they are raised off the ground on blocks to stop them rotting through the base. Pots and containers can be filled with a mixture of high-quality planting fibre with soil, vermiculite and peat, which is lightweight and helps to keep down the weight-load on the roof. Unless you have a deeper area of soil on the roof it will be unlikely that you can grow trees, but some small trees will survive in pots until they get too big.

All too often you see a roof garden with a few dead plants in pathetic-looking pots. To avoid this depressing scenario, choose plants which, in nature, are wind tolerant and choose those that are able

59

Balconies and verandahs

Verandahs and balconies offer a wonderful opportunity for a relaxed, informal design, while creating a useful bridge between the architecture of the house and the form of the garden. Keep the planting simple and the colour palette limited.

ONE OF THE SECRETS in a very small space, such as a balcony, is to try to shift some of the plant material off the floor of the balcony by attaching planters to the railings or to the wall. This not only makes additional use of all the vertical space, it gives you more room on the floor of the balcony itself for furniture.

The smallest spaces are among the most difficult to design successfully, since they demand a rigorous attitude to what is, or is not, included. In a very small space, any mistake is immediately obvious, and every plant has to be chosen with care for its all-round attributes. Ideally for these situations you need plants that will reward you at different times of the year – perhaps with flowers in early summer, good foliage throughout the growing season, and colour in autumn – or at least a planting scheme that has been designed with different seasons in mind. One solution is to change the plants in containers with the seasons, introducing fresh material for spring, summer, autumn and winter, with a big display, say, of tulips and muscari in spring, lilies in summer, chrysanthemums in autumn and cyclamens and ivies in winter.

The most common problem with many balcony gardens, as with roof gardens, is exposure and cold winds. Some kind of screen needs to be erected on the windward side. Trellis or slatted screens can work well or even lightweight metal frames fitted with either glass or perspex can be used. Be careful of weight on balconies, since a projecting balcony cannot support an excessive amount of it. Be equally careful of drainage because water must escape and should not be allowed to build up so that flooding causes problems to rooms below. It is wise to check before creating a balcony garden that the waterproofing and drainage are adequate.

Window boxes

Small areas of carefully thought-out planting can add immeasurably to the look and feel of the overall scheme. On a verandah or balcony, make sure that any windows overlooking the area are used effectively for small, but striking, displays. The container here is as important as the plants themselves, since it is very much in evidence. All too often you see beautifully planted window boxes, where time and trouble has been taken designing planting schemes that have unfortunately been housed in ugly plastic containers. The containers do not need to cost a fortune – you can even recycle old boxes and paint

Tropical paradise
OPPOSITE This lush backdrop provided by palms in pots and tall surrounding trees not only gives shelter from the hot, tropical sun but creates an impression of seclusion and tranquillity. Similar effects could be provided in temperate climates by using identical oriental furniture and exotic-looking large foliage plants, such as *Trachycarpus fortunei* or bamboos.

Sunscreen
LEFT The loggia, with its filtering overhead screen, becomes a comfortable place to sit, day or night. The rusty colour of the terracotta-tiled floor, laid diagonally and with prominent grouting, is picked up in the painted concrete supports for the roof screen, which is sturdy enough to provide good support for climbing plants grown over it.

them in interesting colours – but they must complement the planting scheme.

Although a verandah or porch is probably the ideal place to hang baskets, I have yet to see many that I like the look of, because the ball-shape of most hanging baskets, swinging in space, does not seem to look either natural or attractive. If you insist on having hanging baskets, then at least ensure that the contents blend with the remaining scheme, and avoid the mish-mash of clashing colours so often seen. A wicker basket full of different ivies, with perhaps white busy Lizzies, might look good in the right surroundings. They will also look better if hung in matching pairs.

Verandahs

Verandahs are best suited to a relaxed, informal design style. They create a useful bridge between the architecture of the house and the form of the garden, provided they are well-designed. The materials used for the verandah should provide a link between house and garden. If the verandah leads off the kitchen for example, tiling may be the best choice of floor surface, while decking or some form of wooden surface, which is naturally warm both visually and to the touch, may be better suited for a verandah leading from a living area.

Some verandahs are no bigger than a cupboard, with just enough room to squeeze in a couple of chairs. Others are wide enough to dine on. With smaller verandahs, try to keep the planting off the

floor space, by using wall- or balcony-mounted containers, and grow plants whose bushiness is at the top of the plant, not at the base, so that the floor area is not overtaken by the foliage. Plants trained as standards – evergreens such as privet, laurel or myrtle – are ideal.

To link the verandah to the garden, repeat some of the plants and containers. For example, a pair of marguerites (*Chrysanthemum frutescens*) in terracotta containers can stand at the base of steps up to a verandah, and a similar pair can stand on the verandah itself. Keep the colour scheme simple and strong: containers attached to the verandah railings could be planted with a single species of flowering plants – changed seasonally – and with some handsome foliage as a backdrop.

Simple, but refined
RIGHT A cool purple and white colour scheme for this scalloped, wooden planter fixed to the verandah railings makes an excellent focal point without detracting from the clean and spare lines of the architecture.

Old-style elegance
RIGHT The cane and wicker herringbone-patterned loungers on this Colonial-style verandah reflect the elegant bluegrey and cream tile pattern of the flooring, which blends seamlessly with the stone floor of the terrace beyond.

Here comes summer!
OPPOSITE By incorporating a mass of containers filled with flowering plants, both at floor level and on an antique marble table, the verandah takes on a completely different atmosphere. Containers are invaluable for altering the focus of attention in a garden at different times of the year.

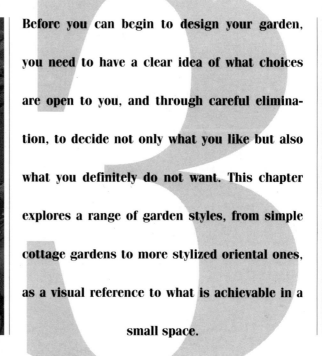

Before you can begin to design your garden, you need to have a clear idea of what choices are open to you, and through careful elimination, to decide not only what you like but also what you definitely do not want. This chapter explores a range of garden styles, from simple cottage gardens to more stylized oriental ones, as a visual reference to what is achievable in a small space.

Styles & situations

• TOWN GARDENS • COUNTRY GARDENS •
• COTTAGE GARDENS • WATER GARDENS •
• ORIENTAL GARDENS • TROPICAL GARDENS •

Town gardens

Although there is nothing to stop you turning your tiny town garden into a wildlife area, to most of us the style term 'town garden' indicates something rather formal. Formality does not have to be boring, however, and there are many ways to create an interesting, and unusual, look for a small urban plot.

WHENEVER I VISIT peoples' homes or travel in cities, I spend a lot of my time nosily looking over walls or peering into a neighbour's garden from a high-window vantage point. It never ceases to amaze me that people do not make the best of their garden space. It seems almost a crime to have a garden in a city or town and to fail to make good use of it.

Planning considerations

Admittedly many town gardens are small, narrow and sometimes shady, and their relationship to other buildings makes them difficult to use because of the lack of privacy. Architects today tend to lack the ability to blend their buildings into the environment, and largely ignore the garden space. However, with a little pre-planning, some careful thought and a logical approach you can turn this space into something that is different, exciting and also adds to your available living area.

Small gardens are among the nicest. Owing to their smallness of scale, they are capable of being fine-tuned and made into attractive, low-maintenance areas, with the minimum of fuss and outlay.

Good planning is the key (which, of course, applies to all garden design), but in a small town garden, viewed, maybe, mostly from one angle – the house – it is important to consider how this view is going to look framed by a window or door.

If garden design does not come easily to you, look at some of the plans for town gardens in the planning chapter, pages 14–35, and then seek the advice of a professional designer or landscape architect to draw you up a plan and give you helpful hints on the way to approach the space you have to offer.

The design of the town garden is usually rather more formal than that of a country garden. However the design principles are the same as those you would use in any other garden, with perhaps more emphasis on privacy and screening from neighbours. Privacy may be difficult to achieve in a space that is overlooked by neighbouring houses or high windows and if this is really a problem then a complete overhead screen, devised in the form of a pergola or trellis work over the top of the whole garden, may be the only solution to afford you some sort of

Foliage framework

RIGHT Further proof that you do not need bright colours for a successfully designed garden. Strong classical shapes in the garden are like good bone structure in a model – they do not need much adornment to look great. Big foliage plants, strategically positioned, give this garden its character, as does the sweeping expanse of the brick paving, neatly punctuated by the curving shape of the bench. This garden is a good example of the principle of less, rather than more, being the secret to achieving balance and symmetry in the garden.

internal space which is private and free from prying eyes. This could then be planted with climbers or even glazed in places to help give added protection to plants below. This would, of course, limit some of the plants you could grow as it would make the garden more shady. Where the space is really restricted and there is little or no usable topsoil, then the town garden is the right place to focus on a container garden. In fact, very often this is a practical solution because you can change the appearance of the garden regularly simply by moving the plants in their containers. I have always considered grass to be an unnecessary addition to a small garden. Usually the space for the lawn is too small to warrant taking up storage space for a mower.

Styles for town gardens

The scale of the space very often has the last word when it comes to style in the town garden. Urban gardens that look like pieces of a country garden in the town usually do not work at all well. If your space is well enclosed and has good protection from

Space invaders
OPPOSITE In tiny gardens, where space is limited, every inch of it must be used to advantage. This scheme relies on pots and containers that can be moved about as the season progresses so that one plant or another plays a prominent role at different periods. Flower interest, in the guise of these 'Stargazer' lilies, is balanced with architectural form, supplied by neatly clipped mounds of box and other evergreen shrubs.

Green tapestry
LEFT Richly varied foliage texture and shape is the key to this planting scheme on a small patio, proving that you do not always need flower colour. Good use has been made of the vertical, as well as the horizontal, space, and this tiny area has an almost theatrical quality, helped by the golden colour of the stonework that acts like a stage set.

weather and neighbours, you can design something lush and exotic, using materials and plants to create a look that has a strong visual impact but that remains functional in its use. A town garden can be an eclectic mix of plants, pots and objects but, provided it is carefully arranged, can still remain very pleasing to the eye. Learning how to combine and blend materials successfully is the basis of good garden design.

Shaping the garden

Creating the right shape is one of the key elements in achieving a permanently pleasing design. The trick is to avoid the irregular curves so commonly seen in suburban gardens and to use instead strong, bold, linear shapes that are then softened by the planting. These strong, simple, basic shapes impose a satisfying geometry on the design which allows you a lot more scope in the more decorative elements of the garden. To decide which shapes to use, take a look at the external architecture of the house and repeat some of these basic shapes in the garden, using bold, architectural plants at strategic points to help build up the geometry. These structural forms will help build the framework of the garden.

As far as the planting is concerned, do not fall into the trap of thinking that the plants should simply fit in around the edge of any hard surfaces. In fact, it pays to turn your thinking inside out and plant the large framework-type plants first, and build the hard surface areas around them.

Choosing the plants

It is important to concentrate on just a few dramatic plants that will work as sculptural contrasts with the strong, hard, landscape forms. Be aware that less is often better than more, and never choose plants because you have been seduced by the flowers. They will, more often than not, be over in a few weeks. It is much more rewarding to think in terms of the plant's overall shape, and foliage colour and form, because it will reward you all year round if it is evergreen.

In a small space it is important to choose plants carefully and well, and to create a good balance between evergreen and deciduous shrubs, and between shrubs and herbaceous plants. As the garden is probably in constant view from the house, one of your main objectives is to have a garden that looks good for as much of the year as possible. A good evergreen framework will provide the underpinning for this, supplemented with some big and worthwhile herbaceous plants for summer interest, when you will be using the garden more frequently. Do not be misled into thinking that because the garden is small, the plants should be small too. A few

A whiter shade of pale
OPPOSITE White is one of the best colours for small, rather shady town gardens as it carries the light and, here, picks up the white-painted walls behind. Variegated foliage, also used extensively here, has a lightening effect in a planting scheme which makes use of every available inch of space.

Tiny jewel
LEFT This tiny backyard, which measures roughly 9m by 5m (30ft by 16ft), belongs to garden designer Tony Noel. It gains unity from its simple green, gold and white colour scheme and the neat rectangle of grass surrounded by York flagstones. Climbers festoon the surrounding brick walls, offsetting the formality with softer shapes and interestingly varied textures and colours.

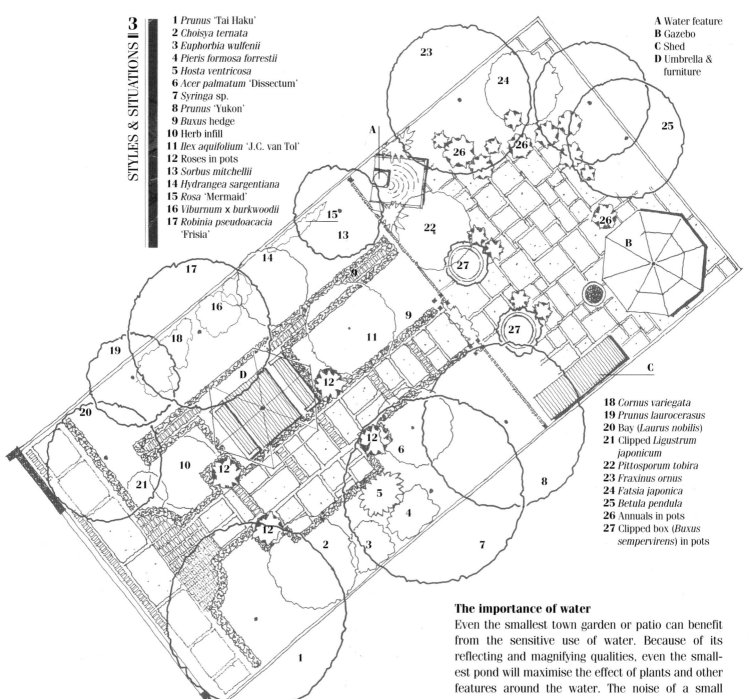

1 *Prunus* 'Tai Haku'
2 *Choisya ternata*
3 *Euphorbia wulfenii*
4 *Pieris formosa forrestii*
5 *Hosta ventricosa*
6 *Acer palmatum* 'Dissectum'
7 *Syringa* sp.
8 *Prunus* 'Yukon'
9 *Buxus* hedge
10 Herb infill
11 *Ilex aquifolium* 'J.C. van Tol'
12 Roses in pots
13 *Sorbus mitchellii*
14 *Hydrangea sargentiana*
15 *Rosa* 'Mermaid'
16 *Viburnum* x *burkwoodii*
17 *Robinia pseudoacacia* 'Frisia'

A Water feature
B Gazebo
C Shed
D Umbrella & furniture

18 *Cornus variegata*
19 *Prunus laurocerasus*
20 Bay (*Laurus nobilis*)
21 Clipped *Ligustrum japonicum*
22 *Pittosporum tobira*
23 *Fraxinus ornus*
24 *Fatsia japonica*
25 *Betula pendula*
26 Annuals in pots
27 Clipped box (*Buxus sempervirens*) in pots

well-chosen large plants in a small garden appear to enlarge the space rather than diminish it, and too bitty and busy a design will certainly have the effect of shrinking it.

Another good reason for creating seasonal interest in the town garden is because, for many town dwellers, the garden is almost their only link with nature. To some extent, an opportunity to watch the processes of nature at work, even if it is only plants unfurling their leaves in spring, flowering in summer, and the leaves turning colour in autumn, is very beneficial to anyone almost totally consumed by the pressures and strains of urban living.

The importance of water

Even the smallest town garden or patio can benefit from the sensitive use of water. Because of its reflecting and magnifying qualities, even the smallest pond will maximise the effect of plants and other features around the water. The noise of a small fountain or perhaps a Japanese bamboo water feature producing a steady trickle into a pool or bowl will add sparkle to a dull patio area. Water introduces life and energy into a town garden.

For really small gardens or balconies, water plants can be grown in large ceramic bowls such as those made in the Far East (usually imported from Thailand or China) and plants like water lilies, reeds or zantedeschias, which flower very well with their roots immersed in water, can add an exciting dimension to the planting. For more ambitious schemes, try something rather more daring and dramatic, as shown in the garden detailed on page 20. Here, the majority of the space has been given over to a water feature around which the rest of the small garden has been moulded. Not only does it transform the garden into a tranquil retreat but it makes the garden look much bigger than it is. Clever planting would distract the eye from its true boundaries while irregular pond shapes can be used to help to disguise the regular square or rectangular shape of the site itself.

Mirrors increase the reflecting capacities of water. Set into a false brick wall or arch, a mirror will create the impression that water flows through the wall and beyond. This type of *trompe l'oeil* will make the garden look much bigger than it really is. Owners of small gardens will very rarely have the opportunity to install a swimming pool in a town but they need not necessarily be totally deprived of this pleasure. Hot tubs or splashpools (see page 186) can take up very little space if well sited and provide a cooling diversion for children and adults in hot weather. Hot tubs can be fitted above ground, avoiding the cost and trouble of excavation.

Lighting

One of the most exciting and dramatic effects that can be created is with lighting. It pays to have a control panel in the house near a window which will give you clear visibility into the garden. You can then set up perhaps two or three different lighting effects using dimmers for the various sequences of lights you arrange. Features such as trees, gazebos, small bridges or water features are all items that benefit

from subtle lighting. It is a good idea to avoid putting too much light onto the boundaries since, if they are slightly darker than the central core of the garden, it will help to make the garden feel larger. Also you do not then run the risk of any light annoying your neighbours. In a really small space, maybe two or three lights are all that is needed. Be careful, too, not to shine lights back towards the house or seating area.

Containers

In a town garden, with limited space and sometimes difficult planting conditions, containers really come into their own, principally because you can move the planting display about when it suits the design to do so, putting one plant into a prominent position when it is flowering, and another, which has finished flowering, into an out-of-the-way corner.

Trees in pots are a good idea for very small gardens. The container prevents the tree from reaching massive proportions, so you can grow a more interesting range, and it gives a different shape and structure to the planting. Japanese maples (*Acer palmatum*) look wonderful in pots, and there is a wide range to choose from, including the spectacular feathery-leaved ones, with purple foliage. If you can afford it, buy a matching pair of these. Also bamboos do very well in pots, making wonderful tall feature plants.

Clever contrasts

LEFT Small-scale, but on classic lines, this little garden designed by Sue Farrell is laid out on a traditional basis with a central path, but the space has been used to maximum effect for a host of shrubs, roses, clipped hedges and plants in pots. The garden is so well screened from neighbouring properties that it appears to be totally private while still allowing enough light to penetrate to grow an interesting variety of plants.

Try, whenever possible, to make sure the style of container suits the design of the garden and that the proportions of the plant match those of the container. Nothing looks worse than a tiny plant in a large container, or a large plant struggling to retain its dignity (and possibly its life) in one far too small.

The very fact that a plant is in a container draws attention to it, and so you must ensure that it is healthy and in good condition, properly staked, if that is required, and pruned, again if that is needed.

Colour schemes

In small spaces, colour becomes a key issue. Although a riot of colour in cottage gardens works successfully in small spaces, this is largely because the flowers used tend to be small and the colours, although brilliant and often clashing, emerge rather like a pointillist painting. If you use an indiscriminate palette of colours in a small space, dotted about round the garden rather than blocked together as in cottage planting, you will make the space look far smaller than it actually is, and very bitty, as your eye is drawn to first one plant and then another. Cool, elegant colour combinations tend to work well – green and white, for example, is a sure-fire winner, and also works well in shade, as many of the shade-loving plants are white- or pale-flowered.

If you do want strong colour, focus it in one place – perhaps on a specific plant, such as one with strong purple foliage, or on a profusion of brilliant coloured flowers in an otherwise more muted colour scheme. Try putting pink and red busy Lizzies, with similarly coloured pelargoniums and orange-flowered daisies, in a group of 'hot' colours against an evergreen backdrop.

Sleight of hand
OPPOSITE This deceptively large-looking garden in fact measures around 8m by 10m (25ft by 32ft), the illusion of space created by Dutch garden designer, Henk Weijers. It demonstrates what can be achieved with clever planting – in particular the contrasting spires of grasses and round-leaved plants like ligularias – a simple pond and a sympathetic surface, like timber decking. Natural-looking, it is nevertheless a carefully conceived and well-executed design.

Big and beautiful
BELOW Heavy shade does not preclude the chance to use interestingly shaped foliage and even small spaces – here 15m x 5m (50ft x 17ft) – can play host to large architectural plants such as *Rheum palmatum*, the impact of which is so great that it makes a living sculptural feature. A shelter belt of trees and shrubs gives protection in overlooked town gardens.

Old favourites

RIGHT This country garden houses a wonderful collection of carefully chosen plants – roses, delphiniums and alchemilla among them. The basic layout gives the illusion of depth, and provides seating space in the sunny pockets alongside the path.

Swags and tails

BELOW Small country gardens require an idea in keeping with their informal style. Here, a metal arch making a corner feature supports swags of clematis and roses, underplanted with cottage-style perennials, including foxgloves, delphiniums and irises.

Country gardens

It is the style rather than the situation that denotes a country garden – loose, informal, and full of plants. You can successfully incorporate, a country-style garden into a town situation, simply by following this formula.

YOU OFTEN HEAR the phrase 'country-style garden', but what does it mean? Possibly it means different things to different people. To me, it sums up gardens with a bit more space than the average urban plot, and where the surfaces and planting are more relaxed and informal than in the typical town garden. For some people, it sums up something even grander – the Victorian-style garden with its wide herbaceous borders, sweeps of lawn, and walled kitchen garden.

Most country gardeners today, even those with small gardens, are obliged to adopt a much less labour-intensive style of gardening. Two of the best concepts for this sort of approach are to use large shrubs and roses underplanted with quick, invasive, ground cover, through which bulbs like lilies and fritillaries can be persuaded to grow, and where any bare soil is covered with bark chippings. The time-consuming and infinitely boring chore of weeding is then largely eliminated and what work there is centres around the more interesting tasks of pruning, shaping and perhaps planting. Lawns can be replaced by less labour-intensive surfaces, such as gravel, chamomile lawns or wild-flower meadows.

Surfaces

Grass can be a chore even in a relatively small space, and in those gardens where space is really limited it is simply not worth having a lawn. Other surfaces do the job better. My favourite surfacing for a country garden is large stone slabs, spaced at generous intervals, and with a fairly irregular juxta-positioning. Small plants can then be encouraged to grow between the stones, colonizing the gaps, so

that the garden takes on a feeling of maturity in a relatively short time.

Gravel is another good surface material in country gardens and old hardwood timbers, whether sleepers, fence or gate posts, or scraps of wood, look well set into it in this relaxed style garden. These, combined with brick or stone paths, do a lot to help counterbalance any harshness that may occur from using just one hard material. Timbers, when grouped tight together into a deck area, make good informal seating areas and can have large plants like *Miscanthus*, *Macleaya* and big silver-leaved thistles (*Onopordum*) to enclose or give some privacy to any sitting space.

Softening effects

Wherever you have hard surfaces in the country garden, you will need to grow plants that help to break up the monotony of its expanse, either interplanted between the stones or grown to spill across them. Those for interplanting have to be small and fairly tough, to survive the occasional crushing underfoot. Plants that release scent when crushed are ideal – the thyme family, for example.

Plantsman's garden
ABOVE This small country garden is brimming with plants, grown either side of the curving path which makes it appear larger than it is. Striking Regalia lilies, standard fuchsias and shrubs make the vertical framework.

Sensuous curves
OPPOSITE Containers in country gardens fit in most successfully when they echo the curving and billowing nature of the planting, like this urn, spilling over with roses. Gravel surfaces are inexpensive to lay and very adaptable. Sun-loving plants help to punctuate the flat expanse.

To spill over the edges of paving, over walls or down steps, you can grow larger plants that have either a mound-forming or trailing habit. Many of the geranium family are ideal for this purpose, as are helichrysums and heleniums (the latter two both doing well in hot, dry sunny situations). Herbs, which also enjoy dry, sunny situations, flourish, including sage, prostrate rosemary and santolinas.

Another feature that is required in these situations is the ability to self-seed freely. Among plants that do so, the little daisy, *Erigeron karvinskianus,* known, with reason, as daisy-gone-crazy, is at the top of my list. It will settle into any niche or crevice it can find, rewarding you with clouds of tiny pale pink flowers in summer, which make a delightful contrast with the formality of stone paving.

Alchemilla mollis is another good self-seeder, and I am particularly fond of its soft green leaves and delicate yellow-green flower heads. Again, it blends beautifully with stone but is best interplanted in areas of the paving that are not used as a thoroughfare or for dining out, as it is a little too tall.

Among the mat-forming softening plants, the various thymes are a must. I particularly like *Thymus* x *citriodorus,* whose tiny leaves are wonderfully scented when crushed. There is a golden-leaved form, 'Aureus', and a silvery white variegated form 'Silver Queen'. Another pretty thyme is *T. praecox* 'Annie Hall' which has pale pink flowers and lighter green leaves than most thymes.

Planting

Although the country garden style is based on traditional ideas of what gardeners did in the past, new-age country gardening can embrace the current passion for things natural with softer, wilder plants and flowers, in a basic framework of low-maintenance trees and shrubs. With this in mind, it is a good idea to make use of some of the bigger plants such as the enormous *Gunnera manicata* with its massive spread of leaves. I have a large one (which came with the house) at the bottom of my garden. I think I bought the house for the plant, and it has been divided year after year to create new progeny.

For fast-growing ground cover to suppress weeds the large-leaved *Petasites japonicus* is ideal, although it can become very invasive, and if the distinctive spotted lungwort, *Pulmonaria* sp., needs an introduction, this is a very good plant for ground cover under shrubs and roses. Green and grey foliage is restful on the eye, and makes the perfect background for drifts of soft, natural-coloured plants, such as the perennial *Ligularia dentata* 'Desdemona', which just happens to be my all-time favourite plant. This produces wedges of tall orange daisy-like flowers which are highly attractive to butterflies. It flowers in late summer and looks much better when planted in large groups – at least five

Good companions
LEFT Choosing plants that go well together is perhaps one of the most difficult aspects of garden design. However, if you limit the number of plants you choose and think carefully about their overall shape first, and their flowers second, it makes the choices easier. It pays to try to repeat themes and forms. Here, the strappy foliage of the sugar-pink flowered *Crinum* x *powellii* is matched by the arching mound of leaves of *Miscanthus sinensis* in the background. Both of these provide a good vertical contrast with the horizontal planes of the deck and the hedge. Another useful trick is to think first about the shapes that are required, and then try to find plants that will create them.

together. *Rodgersia tabularis* is another wonderful plant for moist shade with a huge leaf like a big dinner plate, but its real beauty is its soft apple-green colour, which blends beautifully with other moisture-loving plants like primulas or hostas. These sculptural and exciting plant forms all need to be planted in large groups to gain impact and give form to the garden's overall shape. I always restrict annuals to pots and containers around the edges of the house, where they can be easily cared for and watered. Annuals in large bedding arrangements usually look too well-regimented and municipal for most people's taste.

Vegetables and herbs

Among these soft semi-wild plants it is quite nice to make a small bed for herbs, or even vegetables, perhaps even introducing the odd cabbage or tomato into an otherwise floral planting scheme. Vegetables can be as attractive as any flower, and savoy cabbages produce spectacular curly heads, and look very good as a foil for brightly flowered companions around them. Parsley is another attractive 'foil' plant and looks particularly good planted with blue pansies or orange nasturtiums.

Medicinal and culinary herbs can also be attractive plants in their own right. Consider their design

Edible elegance
RIGHT An ornamental potager garden fits comfortably into a country-style garden. Here, circular beds have been arranged in a practical manner to allow easy access and clever use of space to grow herbs and strawberries (under nets against birds) and courgettes, rhubarb and cabbage in the outer beds. Box edging to the beds and neat brick paths gives a classical feel to the design.

possibilities too. For example, tall bronze fennel, *Foeniculum vulgare*, grows to a height of 1.5m (5ft) and has wonderful, large umbels of deep brown gold flowers. Its dark feathery leaves make a splendid contrast with other more solid-looking foliage plants. It may be necessary to set aside a small area for herbs, fruits and vegetables, which are traditionally the essential elements of the country- or cottage-style garden. Do not reject the idea of edible plants in your plan because they are too much trouble or you do not have room to hide them away. Often they look as good as they taste, and can be as valuable to the garden designer as any other plant. Fruit can be trained against walls, or grown informally in hedges. Raspberries and blackberries could easily be included in a 'tapestry' hedge, oak-leaved lettuces and ornamental cabbages are good front-of-the-border-plants, and runner beans can make temporary screens.

Other attractions

Water, of course, is an essential ingredient in a country garden. If you do not want to go to the expense of building an elaborate pond or formal fish pool, then just a few individual pots, planted with water plants, or some large clumps of reeds in cut-down wooden barrels, make simple but interesting features. Be on the look out for old stone troughs, which, if big enough, make good water features, perhaps placed in the garden where a bamboo pipe can re-circulate water from a reservoir below or a purpose-designed water feature can be made, incorporating the stone trough.

No country garden would be worth its name if it did not attract a good number of butterflies and bees. Among the best plants for doing so are the buddleias. One of the most attractive is the grey-leaved, gracefully arching *Buddleja* 'Lochinch' or *B. fallowiana*, which is slightly less vigorous than the common buddleia. *Agastache foeniculum* looks like a smaller version of a buddleia, with its purple spikes of flowers on a single stem, and is also a brilliant butterfly attractor, seducing tortoiseshells and peacock butterflies in droves. Lavender is a great draw for bees, which will hum in clouds round its deeply scented flower spikes all day long. There are many excellent types of lavender, both large and small, which make attractive edgings when clipped.

Herbs for edging
BELOW A small herb garden in which the plants, including sage, chives, lemon balm and rosemary, break the edges of the central path, while retaining some structure by virtue of being clipped into rounded outlines.

Cottage gardens

A happy mass of plants, growing together with artless abandon, seems to be the universal image of the cottage garden. In fact, it takes skill to create a cottage garden that hangs together well.

SYNONYMOUS WITH old-fashioned species plants, cottage gardens gain their charm from the higgledy-piggledy nature of the crammed planting, each plant jostling with the next for space and attention, so that no single specimen stands out or takes pride of place. In many ways, it is the antithesis of good garden design, where attention is deliberately focussed on particular, prominent features. However, although the cottage garden may lack design clarity, it does not lack charm. The secret is to ensure that most of the ground is given over to plants, rather than surface materials.

The basic framework

The archetypal cottage garden has one central brick path, and a massed array of planting on either side, with very few trees and shrubs. As a result, there is not a lot to look at in the winter and so, for those of us who want year-round value from the garden, some kind of modification is necessary.

Old favourites

RIGHT Pink is the chosen colour, and scent the predominant theme, in this carefully planted small cottage garden, where roses, mallow (*Lavatera* sp.), daisy-gone-crazy (*Erigeron karvinskianus*), pansies, old-fashioned pinks and variegated pelargoniums predominate. At evening time, night-scented stocks and tobacco plants fill the air with delicious fragrance.

Informal planting

BELOW In this garden, loosely arranged cultivated plants have been grown together in an informal jumble to create something of the appearance of a wild-flower meadow. Although maintenance of this type of garden is minimal, it is important not to let it become too overgrown or to let any one type of plant dominate.

One of the most successful adaptations is to create a basic central structure – perhaps a cross – with brick paths and small box hedges to provide a permanent feature and then allow a sprawling mass of plants to spill out and over the confining corset of the evergreen planting and hard surfaces. The occasional softly rounded evergreen – such as rue, particularly the lovely form *Ruta graveolens* 'Jackman's Blue' – helps to add solidity to the planting.

Another is to make a fairly formal sitting area near the house, perhaps paved with old bricks or York stone, or gravel with timber insets, and then allow self-seeded plants to soften the effect and tie in with a massed cottage-style planting in the area beyond. To create some design unity, repeat a few of the flowering groups in containers on the patio.

Furniture should be sympathetic to the style of the planting. More delicate shapes fit better with the soft and billowing nature of the plant forms, but avoid anything too overtly rustic-looking or ornate.

Metal cafe-style chairs and tables would look better than overly decorated wrought iron, and a bleached or limed wooden table and benches would be fine.

Planting for colour and scent

Colour clashes are part of the fun of a cottage garden, but make sure that the flowers are all small, so that no particular colour predominates. Crocosmia is a good subject for the cottage garden, its leaves making a spiky contrast with mounds of daisies or helianthemums. Delphiniums, lupins, poppies, *Crambe cordifolia*, Jacob's ladder (*Polemonium coeruleum*) and verbascums all provide height, as do silvery-leaved thistles at the back of the massed planting. Good plants for massed groups are the day lily, *Hemerocallis*, and no cottage garden is complete without the delicate foliage and flowers of aquilegias.

Boundaries should be obscured as much as possible with climbers, wherever possible grown in combinations, so that a delicate *Clematis*, like

Cottage medley

RIGHT In this Auckland harbour garden, crushed shells from the beach have been used to make the path and old English species flowers have been chosen with care to construct a traditional cottage-style planting, as the detail (above) shows, with its combination of geum, violas, alyssum, Shirley poppies and love-in-a-mist.

C. macropetala is followed, perhaps, by various old-fashioned roses – 'William Lobb' has wonderfully soft, velvety mauve flowers – intermingled with fragrant honeysuckles. Other good roses, particularly for climbing through a fruit tree, are 'Rambling Rector', 'Paul's Himalayan Musk' and 'Wedding Day', all of which have clusters of delicate-looking flowers, although they are vigorous growers.

Scent is a key element in the cottage garden, the confused jumble of different fragrances adding to the charm. Big Madonna lilies have a wonderfully rich scent, and were once a common sight in cottage gardens, where they grow happily among other plants. They do not like being disturbed, and the closeness of surrounding planting prevented such disturbance of their bulbs, while also providing support for the stems. Lavender is another must, both for its handsome mounds of silvery foliage and for its spikes of purple, scented flowers in summer, particularly French lavender (*Lavandula stoechas*)

which is very fragrant. It is such a draw for bees that it helps to create that other essential ingredient of any good cottage garden – the hum of insects going about their business.

Geraniums are a must to flank the edges of paths in the cottage garden, as they make neat, low-growing mounds that soften the hard edges of the path. Good ones include *Geranium psilostemon*, whose shocking pink flowers are a terrific companion for *Lychnis coronaria*, and *G. endressii*, which is a good front-of-the-border performer. Artemisias, veronicas and catmint (*Nepeta*) perform a similar function. Herbs are best grown at the kitchen end of the cottage garden, provided that area of the garden is sunny – a sunny bank makes an ideal home for most of the culinary herbs, including thymes, salvias, marjorams and fennel. Try growing *Calamintha nepetoides*, a scented, white, ground-hugging herb that is ideal for tumbling over a cottage garden wall, and which attracts bees and butterflies as well.

Cheerful profusion
BELOW If cottage gardens are about cramming as many different plants into a small space as is possible, then this garden has certainly succeeded. With its tapestry of carefully chosen low-growing perennials, herbs and small shrubs, it paints a cheerful, relaxed picture using lavender, geraniums, violas, sedums, hydrangeas and the dark-leaved *Rosa mutabilis*. It gains from repeating the same colours throughout the planting, principally deep pinks and mauves.

Water gardens

Plants cannot live without water, and no garden is complete without a water feature of some kind, albeit the tiniest pebble pool. With the advent of butyl liners, ponds are easy to construct and maintain; water features also offer a far greater scope of plants to grow, by creating special damp areas in the garden.

I F LARGE LEAVES and architectural plants are my perversion, then designing water features is my fetish. I can hardly remember a garden where I have not tried to incorporate some form of water into the design unless it was physically impossible to do so. Water is an essential ingredient for healthy growth in plants and I suppose that is why it blends so naturally with the planting, and is part of its charm. It never fails to amaze me what a magnetic pull water has for children and adults alike, who seem to be immediately drawn to its edges. For this reason alone, safety should be a major consideration in any design for a water feature, no matter how shallow, if you have young children.

Natural inspiration
RIGHT A water garden in a town garden does not have to be ornamental or formal. In this small London garden frogs, fish and dragonflies make good use of it, as does the occasional poaching heron. The bold clumps of ligularias, hostas, *Gunnera manicata* and the grass, *Spartina pectinata*, are all among my favourite top ten damploving plants.

Floating islands
BELOW A rock pool is crossed by bold blocks of granite, used as stepping stones, which appear to float on the water's surface like the leaves of the water lilies alongside. A limestone sculpture by Irish artist Noel Scullion adds vertical contrast.

To design a water feature for a small garden, whether it is a natural country pond or a water feature in a town garden, I have always chosen as my guide line the wise words of the doyen of garden design, Russell Page, "How little can I do, rather than how much can I do, to achieve the most telling result." This statement is true of most things in gardening and particularly true of water, which is best kept as simple as possible. Trying to be clever with it, unless you have the extraordinary skills of a water sculptor like Bill Pine is a recipe for disaster (I speak from bitter experience). Water has a high quotient of visual magic, and its reflective qualities and its ability to create a soothing noise if pumped into a receptacle are its greatest assets. The sound of splashing water also helps drown out some of the traffic noise in a town garden.

Placing a water feature

In a small garden it is usually a good idea to position a water feature against one of the surrounding

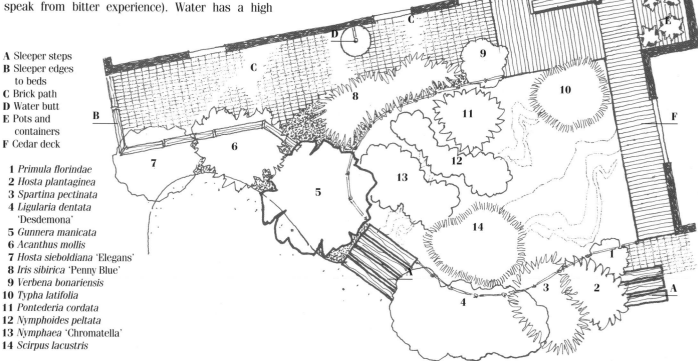

A Sleeper steps
B Sleeper edges to beds
C Brick path
D Water butt
E Pots and containers
F Cedar deck

1 *Primula florindae*
2 *Hosta plantaginea*
3 *Spartina pectinata*
4 *Ligularia dentata* 'Desdemona'
5 *Gunnera manicata*
6 *Acanthus mollis*
7 *Hosta sieboldiana* 'Elegans'
8 *Iris sibirica* 'Penny Blue'
9 *Verbena bonariensis*
10 *Typha latifolia*
11 *Pontederia cordata*
12 *Nymphoides peltata*
13 *Nymphaea* 'Chromatella'
14 *Scirpus lacustris*

Converted cellar

LEFT The small pool in this farmyard was once a storage cellar. It nestles between the farm and the outbuildings, with a decked walkway on one side and strong, bold architectural plants on the other.

Lushly planted

OPPOSITE I like to see ponds crammed with plants. Water is such a lush environment and, if it is richly planted, it will provide a better habitat for wildlife. To produce an air of intrigue, grow tall plants in the water margins. Rushes, like *Butomus umbellatus,* grasses like *Miscanthus,* and irises are all ideal.

Gentle swirl

ABOVE & OPPOSITE This circulating water rill centres on a deep pool in a sunken, circular, granite-paved area. Lush water plants, such as *Iris ensata*, *Lythrum salicaria*, primulas, trollius and *Zantedeschia aethiopica*, are fed by channels from the central pool to create suitably boggy areas in which they thrive. *Butomus umbellatus* and *Pontederia cordata* grow in the water itself. I used old granite setts to line the rill, with a butyl liner under them to create the waterproofing.

walls. This helps to put more emphasis on the perimeter of the garden and leaves the central space clear for seating, entertaining and so on. A large basin or a semi-circular pool against a wall looks good with a spout pouring from a head or mask. With a small pump, you can circulate the water through this, disguising the pipe by fixing it into the wall at the time of construction. One good method of construction is to create the pool in block or brickwork, render it, and then cap the top with tiles or stones. If you add an oil-paint colour such as old terracotta or sienna to the render it gives it an Italianate feel (see the ceramic fish fountain on page 97). Sometimes I tile the back wall of the feature and simply render and waterseal the inside of the pond with a resin.

You should avoid putting your feature in dark shady areas under trees as leaves very quickly foul water and you will be continuously fishing them out. Also water looks so much better when some sunshine can penetrate into its depths. If you want an exciting night-time effect, install some low-voltage dramatic water lights (see page 168). Water pumps are easily installed and can be obtained from your

local aquatic nursery. These are cheap to run as most of them would take up the same electricity as a small light bulb. However, you need to ensure that you have a safe, watertight, electrical supply for any underwater pump.

Planting choices

The perimeters of a pool can be great fun to plant, pots of ligularias, ferns, hostas, lilies and cannas all work very well but arums (*Zantedeschia*) are best planted in pots into the water.

A simple stone basin can be filled with water and pots of water plants such as iris, arums, pontederias, reeds and so forth can be set on stones or gravel with the tops of their pots out of the water. Top the basin up regularly with water in the summer and make sure that the plants are taken out for the winter if temperatures drop below freezing. The same idea can also be carried out with a large and deep Chinese or Thai glazed pot that is waterproof. Plant a large water-lily root in a basket specially made for water lilies, available from your water gar-

den nursery. Place the basket at the bottom of the pot after plugging up any drainage holes with quick-setting cement or a cork. Fill around the lily basket with soil and then put about 10cm (4in) of gravel over the top of all the soil, making sure you do not cover over the crown of the water lily, and fill the pot with water. Reeds, irises and pontederia all make superb subjects for water pots. It is best to choose a small-growing lily which does not put on too much leaf. If you can get hold of the lotus flower (*Nelumbo nucifera*), then this is the ultimate choice for growing in pots. It does need a warm situation – a conservatory or perhaps a greenhouse in winter.

Another simple but very effective water idea is to create a reservoir below ground with a plastic water tank of about 100 litres (8 gallons) or more, over which two concrete lintels are spanned, resting on two concrete supports either side. Over these lintels a heavy duty fine wire mesh is placed and then a large water-worn flat rock, with a hole drilled through, is laid over this. A pipe is fixed through the rock to a pump in the reservoir (it should have a float switch in case the reservoir dries up, which would automatically turn the pump off). Place small round stones around the large rock to cover the rest of the mesh (see diagram).

The only real maintenance required is to top up the reservoir once a week in summer to cope with evaporation, and to brush away any leaves and rubbish that may fall round the water. Tall grasses, reeds or water iris planted in a natural group around this feature make the finishing touch. It is also easy to build a Japanese water spout that can

play over rocks or perhaps onto one big central stone which has a hemisphere carved out of it to make it look like a basin. You could use an old pump or bent copper pipes to create similar ideas based on the reservoir principle in the feature described. A small electric pump is all that is necessary.

Bigger ponds

If you want to keep fish and grow water lilies in a more serious way then a butyl-lined pond would be the best answer. This can be achieved best in a larger country garden where a little more space is available and where the style fits more comfortably with the surroundings. Butyl liner can only be fitted once the shape of the pond has been decided upon and then excavated. It can then be correctly measured and fitted to the actual size of the excavation. If you have a large supply of strong sticky clay, you can dispense with the liner, but creating a pond from clay is not a job for the faint-hearted and you would be better to get professional help and advice from somebody skilled in such an operation. The beauty

of a butyl or clay pool is that a free-form shape can be created providing great potential for lots of planting and a good natural habitat for wildlife.

It is vital not to puncture a butyl liner so it has to be laid onto sand or something similar that prevents stones or sharp objects from piercing it. You can use heavy-duty bubble plastic or, if you have very stony ground, it may be necessary to use sand and then a membrane before laying the butyl liner. Once the liner is in place, then the water level has to be exactly right. Water makes the perfect level and you cannot have one end of the pond higher than the other, as once you've filled the pool with water you will see the edge of the black plastic liner showing above the water level. This looks hideous and will stop you achieving a natural look.

There are various ways of disguising the edge, either with rocks or stones to form a beach, which is very attractive (see page 32), or by bringing soil or turf to the edge, and then either planting it or grassing over it. The other solution is to tuck the liner under a timber edge which requires some careful planning to get right. The water should come up to the timber edge, hiding the liner.

I like to provide a damp overflow area to the pond so that there is a place where bog-loving plants will grow. This also extends the size of the pond because the planting merges the edges into the surroundings. If you are using some form of timber edging, you can make a small platform that cantilevers out over the pool to make an area from which to feed the fish or just gaze at the water.

Maintenance

Keeping water fresh and clean is probably the most important consideration if you have a small water

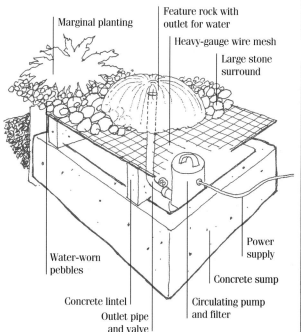

Marginal planting

Feature rock with outlet for water

Heavy-gauge wire mesh

Large stone surround

Water-worn pebbles

Concrete lintel

Outlet pipe and valve

Circulating pump and filter

Concrete sump

Power supply

Coloured rock

LEFT & FAR LEFT A large piece of natural rock, through which a hole has been drilled, makes a simple and safe water feature. The water splashes over the rock, colouring it attractively, and onto the pebbles below, before being recycled through the hidden reservoir.

feature. In a natural pond, the oxygenating plants and the balance between fish, plants and other microscopic creatures should do this for you. In a smaller water feature, with a thin stream of water, you may need to treat the water (if you are not putting fish or plants in) with a sterilizing chemical to keep it clear. This is available in the form of algicides which can be purchased through your local aquatic garden centre.

Oxygenating plants are, of course, the best way of keeping water healthy for fish and these need to be planted well before you put any fish into a small pool so they can establish and so that the water itself has had time to release any chlorine which will be present if you have filled the pond from a tap. This form of informal pool can also be successful where space is slightly limited but it is at its best over a larger area where a good variety of moisture-loving plants can be grown to form a subtle background to the water's surface. It will look after itself, creating its own biological balance, but does require the removal of any dead foliage of water plants, fallen leaves in autumn, and the thinning of species which get too rampant. If you are going to keep fish in large quantities then it may be necessary to fit a filter system to the pond or even an ultraviolet water sterilizer. This will depend on the quantity of water in the pond. You can get advice on this when you purchase fish, or a filter or sterilizer from your local suppliers.

Water plants

Water plants are some of the most exciting by far to grow, not because they have many colourful flowers (although some of the bog primroses are quite exotic) but because of their shape and forms. They tend to have soft, subtle, flower colours, which further endear them to me, even though the bright colours

Recycled for water
ABOVE An old granite animal feeding trough makes an excellent, natural-looking container for a garden water feature, in this case filled with water and positioned in a small, shallow pool.

Water spout
RIGHT Where space is limited, a wall-mounted mask, through which water pours into a small container, may be the best solution. This one is a modern replica of an antique design.

Distinctly fishy

LEFT & BELOW This small, wall-mounted fountain with its fish and ornamental arch was created in clay by Jane Norbury, and painted to look like stone. A pot of *Clivia miniata* dominates the foreground with its brilliant red flowers and glossy strap-like leaves.

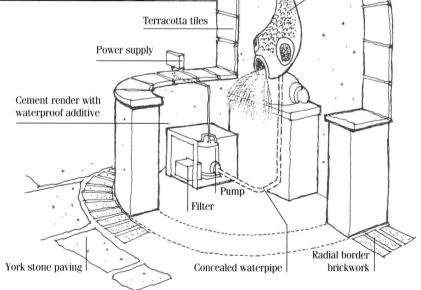

Ceramic fish waterspout

Terracotta tiles

Power supply

Cement render with waterproof additive

Pump

Filter

York stone paving

Concealed waterpipe

Radial border brickwork

of marsh marigolds, primulas and some water lilies are really quite fantastic. For many people water lilies are a must, and who can blame them as they are so beautiful when in full flower and the leaves are the perfect foil for their rose-shaped flowers. However, marginal plants give you the best chance to display a talent for grouping and combining different shapes. The leaves of so many water plants are dramatic and bold, whether in spikes, swirls or delightful giant saucers. To contrast with these there are the tall, strong, vertical shapes of reeds and rushes, irises and pontederias. My favourite rush of all is *Butomus umbellatus* which has starry umbels of flowers in midsummer.

The design potential of such plants deserves a section of its own, and is dealt with on pages 162-5.

Oriental gardens

The skill with which the Japanese approach any element of design is unparalleled. One of the secrets is to keep it simple and structural concentrating on foliage shapes.

AN ORIENTAL GARDEN does not necessarily imply an authentic Japanese garden. In fáct, the principles on which Japanese or Zen gardening are based were developed in China many thousands of years ago. Oriental-style gardens can have various Eastern influences, whether from Japan, Thailand, Malaysia or India. Oriental-style gardens seem to look good in urban settings, where the space is limited and the boundaries clearly defined.

Principal features

For most of us, however, it is fairly easy to translate some of the more accessible principles into a highly

Colour contrasts

RIGHT Oriental gardens fit well into contained spaces, such as courtyards, and can borrow from the principles on which Japanese gardens are designed, without being too narrow in concept. The contrasting yellows, purples, and greens in this scheme are pulled together by the use of similar forms and shapes.

Spiritual welcome

BELOW A Buddhist spirit house, illuminated with night-lights, makes a good corner feature. Who knows what benefits the spirits could bring to your garden!

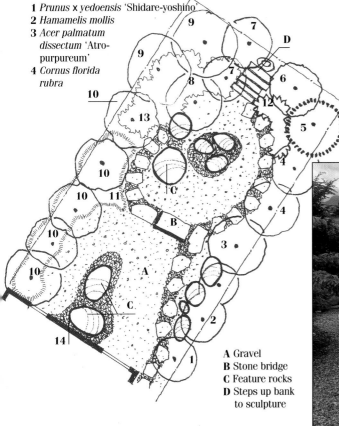

1 *Prunus* x *yedoensis* 'Shidare-yoshino'
2 *Hamamelis mollis*
3 *Acer palmatum dissectum* 'Atro-purpureum'
4 *Cornus florida rubra*

5 *Pinus griffithii*
6 *Ilex crenata*
7 *Cornus kousa chinensis*
8 *Acer japonicum* 'Aconitifolium'
9 *Cornus controversa*
10 *Malus hupehensis*
11 *Miscanthus sinensis* 'Silver Feather'
12 *Hosta ventricosa*
13 *Ligularia stenocephala*
14 *Sagina subulata*

A Gravel
B Stone bridge
C Feature rocks
D Steps up bank to sculpture

Terraced garden
OPPOSITE This intricately formed Japanese garden has made the most of an enclosed, shaded area. The irregular stepped terrace is matched by the small hummock-forming plants, giving it unity.

effective design style of our own. Two of the arts of a Japanese garden are the reduction of scale and that of representation, where a miniature landscape is recreated with rocks for mountains and gravel for sea, and small shrubs for trees.

Ideally every element of the garden should have more or less equal weight, so be careful when adding rocks or boulders not to get them out of scale with the other elements in the garden. To give a more authentic look to such a garden, cover the walls in bamboo screens or reed fences. They provide excellent wind protection, and they are also useful for masking ugly wire fences or unattractive walls. For the surfaces, small water-worn pebbles can be collected, with some rounded, well-shaped stepping stones laid in a random pattern to provide a path from a door, say, to a gate. Raked gravel is another attractive idea, much used in Japanese gardening.

Plants and planting

The plants that we associate with Japanese gardens are azaleas, ferns, Japanese maples, cedars, pines and bamboos but the main consideration is to find plants with good rounded forms and interesting leaf shapes. Bamboos, incidentally, make excellent pot plants, particularly when housed in big Chinese ceramic pots, and the advantage of growing them in pots is that they then do not invade the whole garden, which they are inclined to do, given half a chance. If you do plant them in the soil, you may need to allow time to cut them back annually, dig-

ging around the perimeter of the clump and cutting off any new rhizomes. The dwarf bamboos (*Sasa* sp.) are less vigorous. *Sasa palmata* grows to about 2m (6ft or more) in height, and has a large strong leaf, whereas *Sasa veitchii* is lower growing, with slight variegation on the leaf tips.

For the mossy areas that are often a feature in these gardens, you can use *Sagina subulata*, which is a very fine-leaved carpeting plant that has a tiny white flower, if grown in full sun. For shady areas, *Soleirolia soleirolii* (formerly known as *Helxine soleirolii*) and commonly called baby's tears, is the best option, and will rapidly spread over gravel or moist rocks if out of the sun. Mondo grass (*Ophiopogon japonicus*) is a beautiful small grass that can be used to create soft effects around the base of boulders or around stepping stones. It is not completely hardy, however.

Other good plants for the Japanese style garden are *Fatsia japonica*, *Osmanthus fragrans*, *Pittosporum tobirum*, *Aucuba japonica*, *Kerria japonica*, and camellias and flowering cherries. Around a water feature, plant some of the Japanese irises with their delicate papery flowers, and in the water itself, water lilies – both flowers frequently used symbols in Japanese painting.

Oriental symbolism
ABOVE When designing this rock and gravel garden in Switzerland, I was inspired by Japanese symbolism. Its simple stepping-stone path and islands of water-worn stones could easily be copied on a much smaller scale, but the planting needs to be kept simple, as does the colour scheme, so as not to distract from the graphic nature of the design. The mossy plant between the stones is *Sagina subulata*. The surrounding trees, *Cornus kousa chinensis*, *C. controversa* and *Pinus griffithii*, are all widely used in Japanese-style planting.

Tropical gardens

If you hanker after an exotic garden, then the brilliant flowers, enormous leaves and fantastic forms of the tropical plants and gardens will inspire you to look for similar shapes and colours among temperate plants.

Bold statement

OPPOSITE This tropical house on stilts plays host to large-leaved climbing philodendrons (another good conservatory plant) and offers shade to the patio below, where dieffenbachias and dracaenas have been potted so that they can be moved about. With such dramatic leaf shapes, colour is not important, and this kind of planting style works well in both conservatories and in temperate climate gardens, using large-leaved hardy plants instead.

Exotic leaves

RIGHT The common name for these big-leaved plants is giant's ears (*Alocasia macrorrhiza*) and they are ideal plants for pots in a conservatory, as are the tree ferns behind. If you wish to create a sensuous tropical feeling, then you do need humidity, as these plants are used to a fairly high rainfall and warmth.

VISIONS OF MASSIVE leaves and huge exotic flowers epitomize most peoples' conception of a tropical garden, but, in fact, most tropical plants have few flowers, although the ones that they do have are spectacular. It is perfectly possible, in a temperate climate, to recreate something of the feeling of a tropical garden in a heated conservatory, but remember that tropical plants also require a considerable degree of humidity.

Choosing the plants

The areas of the world in which tropical plants grow are as many and varied as those in which temperate plants flourish. Among the plants we commonly think of as tropical are banana plants, heliconias, philodendrons, ferns, bromeliads (which are epiphytical), orchids, and palms.

One of the first considerations in creating a tropical-style garden is to create areas of shade, not only because humans need it, but because the plants do too. In the actual tropics, overhead screening of some sort is a must – either in the form of a pergola covered in evergreen climbers, or in bamboo or rattan, which can be bought by the roll, or outsize canvas umbrellas. In the conservatory, blinds are essential, as is ventilation.

Tropical plants are quick growing so you need to think any scheme through carefully. Many of the flowers have a very short season of bloom, so you also have to plan carefully to get something of interest most of the year. If you grow orchids, bromeliads and cannas in pots, you can move these into a prominent position when at their best.

Vertical planting is also essential. Climbers such as *Pyrostegia venusta*, the brilliant orange-flowered climber, or *Bougainvillea spectabilis*, the purply-red flowered one, are quick growing and put on a truly spectacular display. Rattan or woven baskets can be hung at strategic points, filled with orchids or ferns.

Design pointers

To design a tropical style garden with any panache, you need an excellent eye for colour and form, using colours in bolder and stronger ways than is usual in

Thai original

LEFT To avoid a sea of green, it is necessary to add plants in pots which can be disguised among the foliage. This garden in Bangkok has orchids, bougainvillea and aphelandra, all grown in pots, and added to the garden when they are flowering. The style of the bird house copies a traditional Thai roof design.

Set piece

OPPOSITE Tropical plants do not have as many flowers as one is led to believe, but the foliage is very exciting and profuse. This tiny New Zealand bush garden has been made on a balcony with the designer's pottery arranged as a still-life.

temperate gardens. The bright light and strong colours of the flowers makes the subtlety of the English country gardening style out of the question. Go, instead, for colour clashes – vivid orange and bright yellow, shocking pinks and scarlets, electric blues with fizzing purples, set off with large, glossy, dark green leaves. For the furnishings, choose brilliantly coloured cushions that will pick up the colours of the flowers, and low tables and chairs, in rattan or cane. Eastern ornaments such as buddhas and carved animal sculptures add authenticity.

Hardy look-alikes

In temperate climates where tropical plants would not survive the winter, you can still create a tropical look for the garden using many of the ingredients of the tropical garden, in terms of the surfaces, ornaments and colours, substituting large-leaved hardy or half-hardy plants for the tropical ones – big-leaved ornamental rhubarb (*Rheum palmatum*), *Trachycarpus fortunei*, and the big magnolia, *Magnolia grandiflora*, for the backdrop, and cannas and lilies in pots, are all possible contenders. Wooden decking, cantilevered out over water, with bamboos in pots, and brilliantly coloured floor cushions and canvas umbrellas, and pergolas festooned with large-leaved climbing plants with big flowers, such as the trumpet vine (*Campsis radicans)* and *Passiflora caeruluea*, will help to recreate the exotic atmosphere of a tropical garden.

The horizontal and vertical surfaces of any garden play a major part in the design, and the choice of style and materials is a key element in the planning of any garden. Mixing different surface types is often the best solution in order to break up the monotony of a large, flat expanse of any solid material. This chapter discusses the range of materials, and the different ways in which they can be combined and blended, or softened by interplanting.

Surfaces

◆ PAVING ◆ DECKING ◆
◆ LAWNS AND SOFT SURFACES ◆
◆ WALLS, FENCES AND SCREENS ◆

Paving

Paving is a major element in most small gardens, and one of the most expensive items in the construction. The choice of materials, and the ways in which they are combined, are crucial to the overall atmosphere.

THE WORD 'PAVING' does not exactly conjure up the idea of excitingly designed gardens, but the hard surfaces are an integral part of the whole garden picture, and need to be considered with great care and sensitivity. The wrong choice of materials can be disastrous, turning the garden into something that more closely resembles a prison yard than an area for relaxation and enjoyment.

There is not much that is new about the range of materials available for hard landscaping in the garden, and the ingredients of the garden have remained the same for centuries – stone, ceramic, aggregate, wood, water, soil and plants. It is, in fact, the way you combine these elements that denotes how successful you are at designing a garden.

The surface materials are a key element in this overall unity, and the arrangements of the paving – the rhythm or pattern on the ground – is more important than almost any other part of the garden because it creates the framework for the planting.

Asymmetrical designs are useful for small gardens where the counterbalance is preferable to uniform groupings of ornaments, plants and urns, or sculpture. A good basic form for the garden becomes a feature in itself, regardless of whether the garden is freezing in the depths of an English winter or baking in an Australian summer. Nevertheless, a small garden has to have a central focus. All superfluous items should be removed to avoid clutter, and the garden should aim to provide a few talking points to add more weight to the overall design. In a small space, it is often better to use only a couple of materials.

Planning the surface

To work out what is required in the way of materials, take the measurements of the area to be paved

Natural perfection
RIGHT Slate tiles have a very special quality – hard-wearing yet soft in appearance – that gives the surface an exciting variation in colour and texture. Here, African and Welsh slate tiles have been combined, the narrower Welsh slate tiles creating a border.

Geometric emphasis
BELOW For a formal garden, tiles and brick paviors have been used in a clean and simple design that gains interest from the change in direction of the pattern at a natural break in the contours. The white grouting helps to emphasize the pattern.

Traditional style
RIGHT & OPPOSITE Brick can be used as a surface material to carry the eye into a space or lead away from it, down a path. Its other virtue is that it is warm in colour, and softer in feel than paving. Billowing plants help to soften the impact.

109

and draw a plan on graph paper to scale. Place the materials or patterns that you wish to use in the form of cut-out bits of coloured paper, also to scale, and lay them on the plan. If this is too theoretical for you, then simply go out and buy the materials you want to use on a sale or return basis, and lay them on the ground in whatever pattern or form takes your fancy. Look carefully at the way the patterns relate to the rest of the garden, and move them about until you feel comfortable with the form. This is an exhausting, but successful, way to ensure that the surface fits well with the overall design of the garden, and can often lead to much more innovative ideas than simply trying to plan it all too rigidly on paper first. Although feasible when dealing with a small area, it would be an impossible operation to carry out for a large one.

Look for materials that have some intrinsic appeal of warmth and colour. Examine whether the chosen material suits the style and form of the architecture of the house. Maybe if you have a red brick house, it would be too repetitive to use brick for the paved areas, but you could pick up the warm colours of the brick in beiges, pinks or terracottas in ceramics, slate or sandstone. If you buy old slates or sandstone, then wash them first with a high-pressure jet before sealing them with a stone sealant.

The house, of course, is bound to be the starting point for any design. The part of the hard surface that lies nearest to it must be as carefully planned as the house itself. I like to work with a detailed plan of the ground floor and examine the way in which doors and windows overlook or give access onto the garden, and where the main areas of traffic

will be. Here the choice of surface is important because it must be practical while at the same time serving aesthetically to link house and garden together. You need to be careful not to make too sharp a change of surface, and if one exists already, then it may be worth creating a small band of tiles that link the interior and exterior together, picking up the colours of indoor and outdoor surfaces.

Paving stones

Formal paving can be jointed with either narrow or wide gaps, and you can work out a range of patterns depending on whether you use regular-sized blocks or random shapes. Expanses of hard surface lend themselves to endless variations of scale. I have always enjoyed laying irregularly sized stone slabs with joints that are slightly wider than normal and

then allowing small ground-cover plants, like prostrate creeping thymes, to grow between them.

When laying stone slabs, they must have a well-prepared, tamped down hardcore base. Allow five blobs of cement (one for each corner and one for the centre) for each stone. When the stones are in position and the cement has dried, grout round each of the stones with sharp sand or fine gravel or grit rather than the customary mortar.

Among the good carpeting plants for shady areas is *Soleirolia soleirolii*, which will spread rapidly in shady, moist conditions. I sometimes use an imported New Zealand plant, *Acaena buchananii*, for slightly taller ground-cover among stones. You can also plant the odd accent plant in among the stones, such as the dark-leaved *Viola labradorica*, another shade lover, or *Alchemilla mollis*, or maybe *Ophio-*

Kerbstone pathway
BELOW These former road kerbstones make a good surface for a path, laid here in gravel. A gentle curve helps to offset the regularity of the stones, as does positioning them at slightly varied angles to each other.

Mossy stones
LEFT Sometimes paving can look much too harsh and monotonous. This circle of irregularly sized and positioned stone slabs has been softened by interplanting with small-leaved creeping plants. Good subjects for this kind of situation are *Sagina subulata*, *Soleirolia soleirolii*, various thymes and *Pratia* sp.

Lawn substitute
BELOW In this garden
the usual geometry has
been reversed, with
the squares this time
comprising a form of low-
growing clover and the
surrounds being cut in
stone. An unusual substi-
tute for a lawn, it would
make a useful surface for
a small front garden, for
example, with a couple of
clipped evergreens in
pots to complement its
formality.

pogon japonicus. The low-growing, invasive, daisy-gone-crazy (*Erigeron karvinskianus*) is another good plant for self-seeding in cracks, particularly in sunny places. It was a great favourite of Edwin Lutyens who allowed it to spill over the stone walls and emerge between the York paving stones of the gardens he designed. Lutyens was a master craftsman with paving and stonework, as many of the great country house gardens he was involved in testify today. Among his superb paving designs were some excellent patterns, using tiles laid on their edge between the stones.

Concrete slabs

Today there are many pre-cast concrete slabs which unfortunately come in sickly greens and mauvish pinks – colours that will certainly clash with almost any planting scheme. Cream or slightly warm shades of grey are less offensive, but if you have to use them for reasons of economy, the most attractive form is a pre-cast slab that is comprised of cement mixed with pea gravel, which is then brushed or washed to expose the aggregate before the concrete hardens, so that the final surface is one of firmly set pebbles. This I prefer to any of the others, but again it should be used in moderation, and possibly combined with another material.

Bricks and sets

Concrete paving bricks are another less than marvellous material, and unless well laid and used imaginatively, they present a severe, almost indus-

Successful links
RIGHT Mixing surface
materials can be tricky.
The answer is to ensure
that either colour or
texture are in common.
Here tiles have been used
to make the connection
between the indoor
surface and the stone
paving outside.

112

trial appearance in a small garden. Good-quality clay bricks make lovely paving but need to be properly laid on a bed of sharp sand, set over a hardcore base. A string course set in cement either side of the path or patio should anchor the bricks and prevent them from moving sideways. Simple patterns are best, and if laid on the diagonal, crossing the garden at 45°, they will give the illusion of an increase in width. Bricks should always be laid on edge as the joint face of the modern brick is ugly.

The old granite or sandstone setts once used for street paving make a very good garden pavement but the small size of the setts is apt to make them look niggly. They are quite a severe surface material and look better with small soft mossy plants growing between them.

Chequerboard

ABOVE LEFT This graphic design has been executed leaving wide margins between the stones, which have then been planted with mondo grass (*Ophiopogon japonicus*). The same idea could be carried out with other plants, such as *Liriope muscari*, *Sisyrinchium californicum* or *Armeria maritima*.

Ancient design

LEFT This pebble pattern dates back thousands of years, copying an Ancient Greek mosaic design. Although time-consuming to lay, the surface is texturally varied. You could alter the pace by creating different motifs within the squares, in stones of varying colours.

Recycled sleepers

OPPOSITE Timber decks can be laid directly onto sand, if the wood is chunky, heavy and well-coated with preservative, like these former railway sleepers. The deck here makes a good contrast of texture with the crazy-paved patio. Sleepers are very durable and require relatively little maintenance – just an occasional brushing over – but they do need washing with a high-pressure jet before being laid to remove any tar or dirt from their surface.

Decking

Wood is a wonderfully soft- and natural-looking material to use for surfaces, and decking not only blends well with most planting schemes but is also surprisingly hard-wearing and durable. With the range of stains and paints available today, it can be finished in any colour you like.

PEOPLE ARE OFTEN nervous of using wood as a surface material out of doors. They think it will rot, or become impossibly slippery, but in fact it is one of the most practical, versatile and attractive surfacing materials there is.

Timber decking adapts itself to almost any style of garden, and one of its great virtues is that it looks good with most other forms of hard surfacing, enabling you to bridge the gap between the house and the rest of the garden smoothly and satisfactorily. No other material can cope so readily with being fitted around trees and other large features, such as pools, or being extended out from the house or over water in the form of a platform or jetty.

1 *Euphorbia robbiae*
2 *Monarda didyma* 'Prairie Knight'
3 *Helenium* 'Moorheim Beauty'
4 *Helenium* 'July Sun'
5 *Onopordum acanthium*
6 *Ligularia* 'The Rocket'
7 *Vinca minor* 'Bowles' Variety'
8 *Crambe cordifolia*
9 *Miscanthus sacchariflorus*
10 *Hosta ventricosa*
11 *Macleaya cordata*
12 *Crinum × powellii*
13 *Campanula glomerata*
14 *Helenium autumnale*
15 *Coreopsis verticillata*
16 *Verbascum bombyciferum*
17 *Digitalis ferruginea*
18 Herbs
19 *Acanthus spinosus*

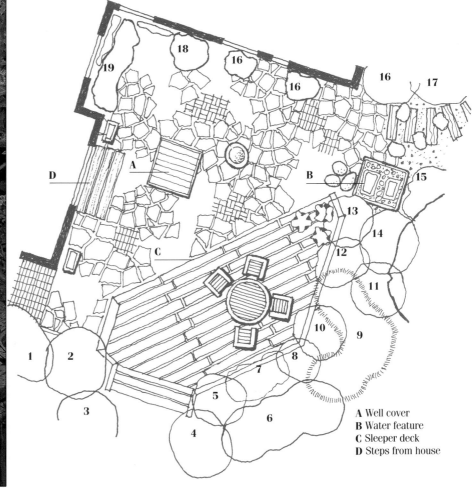

A Well cover
B Water feature
C Sleeper deck
D Steps from house

It is easy to construct. The actual timber strips for the decking have to be laid on battens, so that there is air space between them and the ground to prevent the wood rotting. You can either construct the deck yourself using pre-cut strips of timber and battens, or you can buy ready-made battened sections, which can be laid straight on the ground.

The type of wood you use is important, however. The best ones are hardwoods, which are also the more expensive, but then are extremely durable and require only minimal maintenance: a brushing once or twice a year with a stiff brush and a fungicide, to get rid of any slime or algae growth. Softwoods, such as larch or spruce, can also be used but they will need an annual coating of preservative.

Styles of decking

You can opt for any pattern that takes your fancy, but in a small area it is probably best to keep it fairly simple. It does look attractive, however, if the timber is laid on the diagonal bias, and this will also effectively make any strip of decking look wider.

You can either leave the decking in its own natural wood colour, or you can stain or paint it more or

Wood and water

RIGHT Timber and water make very good companions. It is easy to conceal the edge of a constructed pond by overlapping the timber deck, and its actual structure can be used to anchor the pond's liner. This garden was designed by Henk Weijers, the Dutch garden designer, who rarely misses the opportunity to include water in his designs.

Wood and stone

OPPOSITE, ABOVE Cedar is an ideal choice of timber for decking, as it lasts well and mellows in colour to a harmonious silvery grey, which blends well with most other surface materials. I ran the planking in this design towards the water feature to give the latter more emphasis.

Bridging water

OPPOSITE, BELOW Timber decking is also an excellent means of crossing water. In this garden, the clean lines of the decked bridge make a good contrast with the softness of the planting beyond.

less any colour you choose. The only proviso about using very bright colours is that it is harder to get the planting scheme to blend in.

A nice idea in the right environment is to construct a raised-level balcony, with steps leading down to a timber-decked patio area. Any elevated section of timber must be solidly constructed, with proper fastenings and suitable weight timbers for supporting posts and handrails. Before attempting anything of this nature, it would be wise to seek professional advice and to check what regulations need to be complied with.

Lawns and soft surfaces

Grass is not the only form of soft surfacing. Gravel, timber and bark chippings, or small mat-forming or creeping plants, are all better solutions for most small spaces, particularly if they are shaded.

IN SMALL GARDENS, lawns are rarely the best solution for the surface covering. Not only are they irritatingly labour-intensive to maintain, but few really small gardens have the storage space for a mower. If you want the softness of grass, without the effort, then you would be better off choosing a low, carpeting ground cover, like baby's tears (*Soleirolia soleirolii*) combined with paving stones, or perhaps opting for a small chamomile lawn set into a surrounding hard-surface area.

If you decide you must have a lawn, then its upkeep is critical since it will play a very prominent role in such a small space. Make sure it is properly laid – you are probably better off having it laid as turf – and well fed and watered. At all costs, avoid the sweeping curves and circles so popular for years in suburban gardens. These soft contours are fine in a large park, but they do not fit well into small, tight,

Framed elegance
RIGHT The outline of this formal small lawn in a town garden has been made more interesting by cutting it to fit around the surrounding paved path. By leaving a small but distinct gap between the stones and the lawn, the shape of the lawn is emphasized. Its neat geometry accords well with the clipped topiary and formal pairs of petunias in pots flanking the entrance.

urban spaces, and simply look uncomfortable. It is far better to go for a geometric, but irregular, shape like the one on page 71.

Other soft surface materials

Soft or loose materials such as gravel, sand, and timber or bark chippings are becoming increasingly popular for creating a softer yet reasonably hard-wearing surface for pathways and walks. They tend to look particularly good when combined with timber structures, such as decking, summer houses or pergolas, or an area of trellis.

Mixing materials within a garden design can be very effective for breaking up larger surface areas, but it is important not to mix too many types. Combining more than two or three shapes and

colours, even of the same types of material, tends to make the area look too messy and confusing.

Stepping stones

Stepping stones across any surface, wet or dry, seem to offer an irresistible temptation to cross. It may be a zigzag of stones across a lawn or over gravel, or log rings through a sea of bark chippings, but there is always the unmistakable impression that you are being led somewhere exciting. Safety insists that the stones should be large enough to stand on, and spaced comfortably for stepping onto. They should also be level, stable and non-slip. There are many types of material to choose from. Paving slabs, pavers and even wooden boards are all suitable. You will need to experiment to get the layout just right, and remember that a straight line rarely looks as good as a staggered or winding design. You can use them to break up larger and more severe paving forms or biggish areas of gravel.

Gravel

Gravel has become very popular with certain garden designers. However, like brushing dirt under a carpet, they tend to use it to hide all manner of sins.

Alternative surfaces
BELOW Many gardeners are realizing today that grass is not the only medium for a soft surface, and, for areas which do not get a lot of traffic, substitutes such as thymes, chamomile, *Acaena* or *Pratia* will all carpet the ground with soft green cover, and will require almost no maintenance. Traffic can then be kept, as here, to stepping stones in a path.

There are a few rules that one should stick to when using gravel – look for a nice warm colour (water-worn, round pebbles are better than the chunky browny-yellow type of shingle) and try to break up visually any large expanses of it. I like creating small, winding, gravel rivers that form patterns through flower beds, or putting stepping stones in the gravel. It is better to use this surface material where you can combine it with the right type of planting – maybe cacti or succulents – as it can look hard or unfriendly, particularly in the winter where there is no planting coming through it.

Gravel has been traditionally used in oriental gardens, but I feel that it should really be used only when it can be graded and shaped nicely, and where the form of the gravel has some interest, rather than spreading it from boundary to boundary in one large expanse of boring surface.

Soft surrounds
ABOVE RIGHT Steps, surfaced with gravel and edged with timber risers, make a less hard-looking feature than stone or brick. Here, they are further softened by allowing grasses and alchemilla to spill over the surrounds. Maintenance of gravel is simply the occasional brushing, and the removal of weeds.

Gravel for grass
RIGHT In this small walled country garden, gravel has been substituted for grass. It is a useful surface material which is both low maintenance and inexpensive. In addition it also provides a useful mulch, keeping the roots of plants cool in sunny areas. As a result, it provides the ideal home for shallow-rooting plants like euphorbias, ceanothus or cistus.

Eclectic mix

ABOVE, LEFT This curious combination of *tapis vert* and parterre would reproduce well on a smaller scale in a formal town garden where it would require a surrounding clipped box hedge, perhaps, to separate it from the rest of the planting. Designs like these often look best when viewed from above.

Coloured stones

ABOVE, RIGHT Stepping stones set in chunky gravel provide a natural textured surface where the emphasis is placed on the colour of the stone and the plants play second fiddle.

Minimalist surface

LEFT In this view of the garden seen on page 40, large boulders are surrounded by a river of grey gravel. In a design like this, grass would look out of context and paving too hard-edged and conventional.

Textured terrace
OPPOSITE This steeply
sloping site has been
terraced with expanses of
white-painted wall. The
trees, and the trellis fixed
to the top wall, have a
practical as well as
aesthetic value, giving
privacy and shelter to the
garden above.

Bright topping
BELOW, RIGHT Slate makes
an excellent walling
material as its colour
deepens and changes in
wet weather, and it is
also extremely durable.

Colour statement
BELOW Painted terracotta,
these walls have been
left bare of planting to
increase the architectural
impact made by both the
strong colour and the
cut-out shapes.

Walls, fences and screens

The surrounds to the garden are an integral part of the design and should be considered as part of it. Walls and fences also have a valuable role to play in providing support for plants, while screens give the garden an air of seclusion and intimacy.

EVERY GARDEN needs to be enclosed in some way, and most of us inherit the boundary walls or fences with the garden, and tend not to think about them, unless they require repair or restoration. They do play a significant part in the overall design of the garden, and their contribution should not be overlooked, particularly in a small garden, where they are visible from the house.

Boundary walls

In the confines of a small garden, the boundary wall or fence will be extremely noticeable, and you need to learn to use the space to your advantage. Do not expect the design of the garden to compensate for a poor-looking fence. It will not. However, you may wish to disguise the finite edge of the garden as much as possible to give the illusion of greater space, and you can do this by clothing any vertical surface with climbing plants. The other point to make is that if you are planning to build a new fence or wall, do consult your neighbours and check your legal position.

Another factor that is worth considering is whether the existing wall or fence is high enough to afford the privacy and shelter required. There are legal limitations on height, however, and if you are increasing the height of an existing fence, check with your local authority that you are not contravening any by-laws. If you do need to increase the privacy offered by an existing fence or wall, there are various choices open to you. You can add trellis to the wall or fence, and grow climbing plants up it, or you can plant tall shrubs or small trees in front, to provide additional privacy. In a small garden, you would need to be very careful in your choice of any trees, otherwise your garden would rapidly become very shady, and again you may need to check that you are not infringing on your neighbour's rights to light. Silver birches, some of the flowering cherries, crab apples and hawthorns are all possible subjects for the boundaries of a smallish garden, as are a number of the taller shrubs, such as *Cornus mas*, some of the *Eleaegnus* species and most of the buddleias.

For clothing the walls themselves, there is a marvellous range of plants to choose from, both evergreen and deciduous, some of the best of which are discussed in detail on pages 152-5. Most climbers will need some kind of support, apart from those like ivy that have aerial roots and can cling to any surface, no matter how smooth. The others will need either trellis or wires to twine themselves around. Any trellis work should be fixed to the wall

Traditional brick walls
RIGHT If you are lucky
enough to have old brick
or stone walls in good
condition, their shelter
often makes the ideal
place for growing sun-
loving or slightly tender
plants. Here the pineapple
broom, *Cytisus bat-
tandieri*, gets some pro-
tection from an old wall.

Country craft
RIGHT Although dry stone
walls are usually asso-
ciated with country or
cottage gardens, surpris-
ingly enough they look
equally appropriate in an
urban setting. The con-
struction of fine slivers of
stone requires patience
but the result is well-
worthwhile.

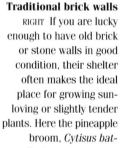

or fence with at least 2.5cm (1in) of air space
between the trellis and the wall. It also pays to use
hinges and clips for the trellis so that you can, if
needs be, detach the trellis from its mounting, complete with its covering of climbers, to maintain a
fence or wall. Hinges at the base of the trellis and
clips at the top allow you to fold the trellis flat while
you do the work.

Other plants, such as most climbing roses, will
need to be tied in if grown over a wall. The big
scrambling roses, like 'Kiftsgate' or 'Paul's Himalayan Musk', need this support on walls, but will use
their long backward-pointing thorns to cling to other
plants if grown into or over them.

Ugly walls, for example plain cement blocks, can also be painted in more attractive colours. Dark green is a good choice, as the foliage of the planting grown over it will blend with it, making it much less obvious. In a shady garden, particularly a basement or one surrounded by high walls, it may be worthwhile bringing in some reflected light by painting any walls white, or at least a very pale colour, and in small gardens, mirrors can be attached to the walls to give the illusion of greater space (see page 198).

Low retaining walls

Gardens on a sloping site often need some kind of terracing to make the slope workable, and in this case a retaining wall or walls will be needed. Ideally they should be constructed in materials that are sympathetic to the area, and any other hard surfaces in the garden. Remember that the weight of the soil, particularly when sodden with water, is colossal and walls for this purpose have to be very solidly constructed if they are to function properly. If in any doubt as to whether the wall is suitable to contain the weight behind it, consult an expert. In all cases, water must be able to drain through the wall, and if the construction is solid, drainage holes will need to be incorporated in the base.

The tops of retaining walls makes ideal places to grow some of the smaller plants that enjoy dry, sunny conditions, and if you choose plants that have

a tumbling habit, they will soften the contours of the walls, and help remove the harshness that you tend to get with any newly built wall.

Fences and railings

When it comes to choosing fencing material, you need to decide whether you want close-boarded fencing for privacy or a more openwork type. For

Temporary fixture
LEFT Many fences are best used only for security and privacy while waiting for planting and hedges to grow. Here this simple wooden plank fence has a newly planted hedge in front of it of quick-growing *Cupressus x leylandii*, which will be cut above the fence to screen the wall behind.

Shelter belt
LEFT Bamboo screens or fencing are best prefabricated in panels, with their construction detail at the back, giving the impression that the fence is a continuous expanse of linked canes. Originally used in oriental gardens, they are particularly useful in small gardens to create compartments or shelter around a patio, for example.

close-boarded fencing, avoid the slightly tacky look-ing pre-fabricated larch-lap wooden fences. They are not suitable unless completely disguised by plants, and they are usually not strong enough, or suffi-ciently durable, to support any real weight of planti-ng. Properly constructed timber fences, with planks battened horizontally, are a far better solution. Interference fencing, which has boards nailed either side of supporting posts, gives an acceptable amount of privacy and offers less wind-resistance than close-boarded fencing. All fencing needs to be well anchored and supported, and remember that the supporting posts must be sunk sufficiently deep into the ground to make a firm foundation or the fence will blow down in the first gale. Any timber supporting posts must be bedded in concrete or fixed into metal support posts. A fence 2m (6ft or so) high must have post holes 75cm (30in) deep.

Where privacy is less of an issue, simple wooden railings or picket fences are very appealing. They make good graphic patterns and have an endearing simplicity about them. You can go to town on these with colour schemes, the best solution being to match it to the paintwork on the house in some way, perhaps picking up the colour of the front door. For temporary fencing, the best solution is split chestnut paling linked by strands of galvanized wire, which is cheap but not unattractive.

Panelled surrounds

OPPOSITE For temporary screening, rolls of bamboo panels are simple and inexpensive to construct, and are useful for pinning over an unsightly fence or wall to give a uniform appear-ance. The lifespan of bamboo is about three to four years, but reed panels, which last a lot longer, could be used instead.

Supporting role

LEFT Wire netting can be left bare where it provides a wonderful support for climbing plants such as roses, clematis, jasmine and wisteria. This soft mix of colour comprises Rosa 'Paul's Himalayan Musk', *Chrysanthemum frutescens* grown as small standards and *Cosmos* 'Sensation'.

127

Oriental screens
ABOVE If you have a feature that you want to highlight or protect, like this Japanese deer scarer (*shishi-odoshi*), a bamboo screen makes an ideal choice of backdrop. To ensure that this little Japanese area looks authentic, great trouble has been taken to tie the knots in the reed screen in the traditional Japanese manner.

Soft blend
RIGHT A similar paint treatment has been given to the trellis and furniture in the garden, where the bench and wooden trellis have been painted the same shade of sage green. Soft colours like these blend much more successfully with the planting scheme than does brilliant white, for example.

Metal railings are often useful for front gardens in urban settings. Old-fashioned metal railings can look rather severe but some modern designs are really excellent.

Screens

Most gardens, even very small ones, benefit by having parts of the space screened from view, because it not only increases the illusion of size if you cannot see the entire expanse of the garden at a glance, it also enables you to incorporate a change of style.

Trellis has many advantages as a screening material, and can also be used to add privacy to existing walls or fences. A trellis cap to a wall is also a security measure since no intruder would wish to climb over it, and trust their weight to its rather flimsy construction. Pre-fabricated trellis panels are a lot less satisfactory than purpose-made trellis. Not only are they less sturdy, but they are often sold in dull-coloured stains. Although the pre-fabricated kind can be used to support climbers on a wall, when it comes to free-standing trellis screens, you would be well advised to create your own, or get a carpenter to do it for you, as it will need to be reasonably strong, particularly if it has to support the weight of climbing plants. For this purpose, the timber frame should be at least 2.5cm (1in) in section, and the timber itself should have been pre-treated with preservative. You can choose the shape of the pattern – square, rectangular or diamond-shaped – but on the whole the smaller the pattern, say 15cm (6in) diameter, the better it looks. Red cedar is ideal for this purpose, if you can afford it, but any soft wood you use must be properly coated with preservative. Today, there is a fascinating choice of colour stains, so be adventurous.

Trellis can also be used in other ways to add interesting features to the garden (see page 198), but it really comes into its own when screening off parts of the garden from view. Remember, however, that a trellis covered in a strong climbing rose, for example, can act as a sail in high winds, and you must make sure that it is properly anchored.

Bamboo and reed panels make excellent screens, and you can get similar constructions in hazel, heather, brushwood, and willow, in various patterns. In a small garden they can either be used in front of existing poor fences, to disguise them, or to screen off portions of the garden, or to afford some shelter for a sitting area. Some are more durable than others, but even the most basic will last for about five years. Again, they will need to be fixed to proper supports, but as they are naturally light and do not provide complete wind resistance, they require less in the way of support.

Gates

Do not ignore any entrances to the garden – as discussed on pages 42-7, the entrance is your first impression of it. The construction and style of any gates is an important part of the whole picture. False gates can be used successfully in a small garden to give the illusion of space. In a small garden, a gate can be used as a frame, focussing attention through an opening.

Purpose and setting will determine the size and height of the gate, but its style and materials must blend in well with other garden features. Wooden gates look fine in both formal and informal settings, but metal gates often need to be given a more substantial surround.

Light and airy

ABOVE In a similarly oriental vein, this slatted fencing is both practical and aesthetically pleasing, as it provides privacy and allows light to filter through it.

Uniform colour

LEFT In this small front garden, unity of design has been created in what might otherwise have been a rather bitty design by painting the metal railings and wooden trellis the same shade of blue. Two bollard-style lights have been fixed discreetly to the gate posts, and painted a matching colour.

129

It is the plants that bring the garden to life, adding atmosphere, colour and interest to the underlying structure. For many people, this is the hardest part of garden design to get right. This chapter provides a guide to some of the most outstanding plants for particular situations – for shade, for sun, for water and for containers, for example – as well as some pointers on how to create planting for maximum impact.

Planting

♦ INTRODUCTION ♦ PLANTS FOR SHADE ♦
♦ PLANTS FOR SUN ♦ EXOTIC PLANTS ♦
♦ ARCHITECTURAL PLANTS ♦
♦ SCREENING PLANTS ♦ CONTAINER PLANTS ♦
♦ MOISTURE-LOVING PLANTS ♦

Introduction

Large leaves, bold shapes and strong architectural form distinguish the plants that make the most impact. Do not let the small size of the garden deter you from using large perennials in your planting schemes.

PLANTING a small garden is probably the most important, if not the most exciting, aspect of the whole design process. You should approach the planting from an architectural viewpoint, the first concern being the form of the planting. It has to have a structural feel and be the right volume for the garden, although it may take time for the plants to grow into the space to achieve this end. In a small garden every planting detail is recognizable and the plant shapes will play a leading role.

It pays to start the planting design by choosing a small tree with strong bold leaves – *Paulownia, Catalpa, Magnolia, Idesia* and *Clerodendrum fargesii* are some of my favourite species. For rather larger gardens, you can try *Populus lasiocarpa, Davidia,*

Living palette
LEFT Perennial planting is probably the greatest fun in gardening. It is like painting with a palette of many colours. Rich colours, such as those of the heleniums here, need a foil of soft grey-leaved plants such as thistles, macleayas or ligularias as a background.

Subtle shifts of colour
BELOW Soft pastel shades work best when planted *en masse*, using small-flowered perennials, with occasional punctuation by grey-leaved plants. Subtle gradations of colour have been achieved using more than one of a particular species.

Aesculus indica, Sorbus mitchellii, S. kashmiriana, or *S. magnifica.* All these trees can be grown in a small garden, provided they are kept pruned back when they reach a more mature size. Most trees can be prevented from getting too large with some surreptitious pruning, provided this is done with skill and with the benefit of some good advice. Where more space is available, I would choose perhaps two of these species or maybe a third of another species, but I like to plant two of the same species of tree where possible. *Sorbus* look well with grey foliage schemes, and *Catalpa* and *Paulownia* look good with large-leaved plants such as *Rheum palmatum, Ligularia* or *Rodgersia.*

I then choose the shrubs depending on the soil type and aspect. For shade, of course, viburnums are an important plant, as many have scent, good leaf shape and can cope with dry conditions. *Hydrangea sargentiana* is a great plant for a more sheltered garden, but needs a reasonable amount of moisture to do well. The rhododendron species, such as Loderi, if you have room and acid soil, *R. macabeanum* and *R. falconeri* (if you can find it) are all wonderful big-leaved species that look superb grown in pots around the base of a large tree. I am not keen on the hybrid rhododendrons and avoid them in my planting schemes.

Plants for special situations

The most valuable plants for shady and dry gardens seem to me to be mahonias. *Mahonia japonica* is a wonderful shrub which never seems to fail, and its

Big and small
RIGHT This sheltered country garden provides a good illustration of the type of plants that you can grow in a small space. Height is an important aspect for containment and intimacy, achieved here with *Cynara cardunculus, Miscanthus sinensis* and *Crambe cordifolia* (shown in full flower). Plants between the stones soften the harsh edges of the paving – in this case, *Alchemilla mollis,* fennel, lavender, verbascum and *Iris germanica. Libertia grandiflora,* growing in the foreground, does best in a warm sunny place. The plan opposite shows the planting in detail.

scented flowers are a joy to behold in late winter. It would be unfair to leave *Fatsia japonica* out of any planting scheme. This hard-working soldier of a plant is such a useful character to put into a garden that has little light. It looks wonderful if planted next to *Sasa* bamboos, a combination that gels in the right association.

Enkianthus sp. and *Azalea pontica* (not to be confused with the rampant *Rhododendron ponticum*) are other plants I use for spring colour but in most cases I look more for perennials with large leaves rather than too many shrubs as the flowering season of the latter is too short, and their interest wanes after a very short period of time. In warm, dry sunny gardens, it is harder to put this concept into practice. Some plants that do work in this situ-

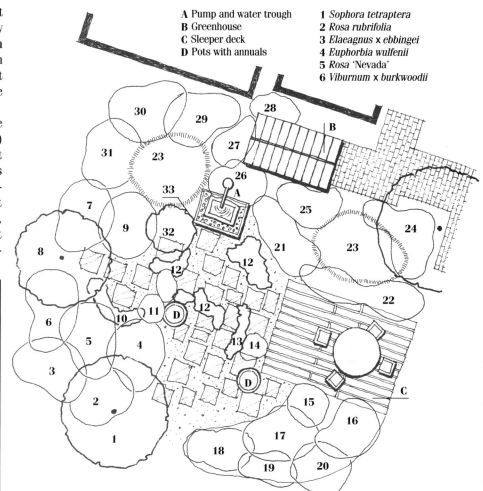

A Pump and water trough
B Greenhouse
C Sleeper deck
D Pots with annuals

1 *Sophora tetraptera*
2 *Rosa rubrifolia*
3 *Elaeagnus x ebbingei*
4 *Euphorbia wulfenii*
5 *Rosa* 'Nevada'
6 *Viburnum x burkwoodii*
7 *Viburnum carlesii*
8 *Sorbus hupehensis*
9 *Euphorbia griffithii* 'Fireglow'
10 *Iris germanica*
11 *Verbascum bombyciferum*
12 *Alchemilla mollis*
13 *Lavandula angustifolia* 'Hidcote'
14 *Thymus x praecox*
15 *Kniphofia* 'Bees Lemon'
16 *Hemerocallis lilio-asphodelus*
17 *Coreopsis verticillata*
18 *Euphorbia robbiae*
19 *Acanthus spinosus*
20 *Aster x frikartii*
21 *Cynara cardunculus*
22 *Verbena bonariensis*
23 *Miscanthus sacchariflorus*
24 *Ligularia* 'Gregynog Gold'
25 *Macleaya cordata*
26 *Ligularia* 'The Rocket'
27 *Crambe cordifolia*
28 *Rosa longicuspis*
29 *Telekia speciosa*
30 *Buddleja davidii*
31 *Rosa moyesii*
32 *Rheum palmatum*
33 Self-seeding verbascums

ation are big, juicy-looking cannas, which grow so beautifully in pots, and can be grown in colder climates if kept under protection in the winter. Daturas (*Brugmansia* sp.) can also be treated in the same way, and look terrific next to tall grasses.

Believe it or not there are some half-hardy banana plants, such as *Musa acuminata* or *Ensete ventricosum*, which come from temperate parts of the world and will be reasonably hardy in a protected garden, if shelter is provided and some winter cover is offered. They are ideal subjects for containers and can be over-wintered in light shade if you do not have a greenhouse or conservatory. For warm gardens and dry conditions one plant with massive leaves is *Tetrapanax papyrifera*, the rice-paper plant, which is a good subject for a sheltered corner. It does not need full sun, and can regrow from its roots if cut down by frost. It is best to give it, like the bananas, some winter protection with sacking or bubble plastic. Its leaves look splendid as a foil against echiums or bamboos.

Plants with good form

Plants with hand-shaped leaves, such as *Rodgersia* (now *Astilboides*) *tabularis*, have a wonderfully sculptural appearance. *Rodgersia tabularis* is a perfect foil for 'Candelabra' primulas and has superb

dinner-plate-sized leaves, produced in the softest of apple greens. It likes damp soil, and light shade, but thrives in a well-protected, not-too-sunny situation, with retentive soil. *Rodgersia* has some other interesting members in its family, but the one that I like best is *Rodgersia podophylla*, a large plant that makes a striking feature under shrubs. It has superb bronze leaves in early spring, turning later to a dull green, with a white plume-like flower in midsummer. In the same vein and also successful as weed-suppressor is *Peltiphyllum peltatum*. Although this plant prefers to be at the edge of a pond, where its roots seek out water, it can also be grown as successful ground cover in light shade, provided sufficient moisture is provided.

Petasites japonicus and *P. hybridus* are normally too invasive for small gardens unless contained by an artificial membrane dug into the ground to stop them spreading into other plants. However, they have extremely beautiful leaf shapes and are ideal specimens for the edge of a pond. My wife calls them poor men's gunnera, and in many ways they are just as dramatic as this stately plant. Another invasive but good strong woodland plant is *Trachystemon orientalis*. This plant is invaluable because of its habit of growing in dry shade.

The new hybrids in the hosta family are very confusing, with their strange names, and I have immense trouble trying to recognize which is which. I stick to my old favourites – *Hosta sieboldiana* 'Elegans' is beautiful, as is its close relative, *H.s.* 'Frances Williams', which has streaks of lime, like an exotic cocktail, through the leaves. *Hosta ventricosa* is an exquisite plant, and needs very little introduction to hosta lovers, but the lesser known *H. plantaginea* has scented white flowers in late summer, and is a wonderful plant.

Another plant that grows well with macleayas is the cardoon, *Cynara cardunculus*, again up to 2m (6ft plus), with grey, finely dissected leaves, and bearing big, blue, thistle flowers that contrast beautifully with its foliage. It does need full sun and plenty of space to grow, as does *Onopordum acanthium*. This enormous thistle is a wonderful foil against other blues, pinks and greys, and can be used as a feature plant amongst smaller-leaved ones. The leaf colour of *Onopordum* makes an excellent backdrop for *Allium giganteum*. This onion bears purple flowers the size of tennis balls on long thin stalks. Its only drawback is that the foliage tends to die back early, making a bit of a mess at low level.

Ferns and grasses

No planting scheme is complete without ferns. These charming plants seem to add a natural touch to any planting arrangement and are best used in small groups around the edges of beds or along the side of a path, where the erect structure delineates and helps to improve on shapes of corners. For damp conditions, *Matteuccia struthiopteris* is one of the best of the ferns, standing up to 1.5 cm (5ft) tall in good conditions. Its common name is the shuttlecock fern because of its funnel shape. There are many varieties of fern, but if you can get hold of any member of the *Polystichum* family, you will be rewarded with some of the most attractive ferns there are. *Polystichum setiferum* or *P. aculeatum* are just two members of the family that have very attractive leaf shapes.

As with ferns, grasses, too, add a naturally bold look to planting schemes and the two that I am most impressed with are *Miscanthus sacchariflorus* and *Spartina pectinata* 'Aureomarginata', the latter prefering damp, moist, situations. *Miscanthus sacchariflorus*, however, will grow in a warm, dry garden, provided it is given enough water during summer months. It is best planted in large drifts where its tall foliage can make a real impact.

Working together

OPPOSITE Old-fashioned roses are great subjects, not only for the impact of their flowers but also for their scent. Quite short-lived in flowering, they are best situated with other plants that will take over the limelight at other seasons. Here *Rosa* 'Celeste' has been combined with *Allium christophii* and hostas.

Leafy contrast

BELOW The impact comes from the foliage combination of *Hydrangea sargentiana*, *Sorbus mitchelli*, box, hebes, and other shrubs.

Plants for shade

Acanthus mollis
H: Up to 1.5m (5ft)
An architectural perenni-
al, with deeply cut, dark
green leaves and hooded
purple and white flowers
in late summer. It needs
plenty of sun and well-
drained soil.

Alchemilla mollis
H: 45cm (18in)
A really good stand-by
plant, alchemilla will
thrive in partial shade.
Forms wonderful mounds
of soft light green leaves,
and in summer produces
feathery sprays of green-
ish-yellow flowers.

Daphne odora
'Aureomarginata'
H: 1.5m (5ft)
Bushy evergreen shrub
with small glossy, yellow-
edged leaves and fragrant
pink flowers in winter.

RIGHT *Hosta sieboldiana*
'Elegans'.
BELOW *Rheum palmatum*
behind *Rodgersia pinnata*
'Irish Bronze' with leaves
of *R. podophylla*.
OPPOSITE Mixed planting of
geraniums, foxgloves,
lungworts (*Pulmonaria*
sp.) and hostas.

Although shade is often considered a 'difficult' situation, there is, in fact, a surprisingly wide range of plants that thrive in relatively low levels of light, although most of them tend to be small- or pale-flowered.

To MANY NOVICE gardeners, shade presents an insuperable problem. They make various hope-less attempts at planting the normal range of plants, and give up in despair when the plants give up on them. Shade is not the bugbear it is common-ly supposed to be. In fact, it offers one distinct advantage – it has a dramatic intensity that can be

put to very good use in design terms, particularly if only part of an otherwise sunny garden is shaded – such as a long, shadowy, alleyway that runs up the side of a house.

The key point to grasp is that certain plants will do very well in shade, and provided that you are dis-

ciplined enough to stick to those that actually enjoy these conditions, you will have a successfully planted shade garden. You will not, however, be able to grow the sun-loving, silver-leaved Mediterranean plants, and your colour scheme will be subdued to predominantly greens, creamy yellows, white and other pale colours. Brilliant flower colours, on the whole, demand bright sunshine. You can always cheat a bit, though, and plant up a container with bright busy Lizzies that grow well in low light levels,

and add the odd hot spot to a shade garden, but on the whole the benefit of shade is the monochromatic colour scheme, in which the emphasis is on the structure and shape of the plant.

Of all the shade-loving plants, ivy is probably the most useful. For a start it tolerates extremely low light levels, and it comes in many forms with a wide variety of exciting leaf shapes. Be warned, though, that you will not be able to grow the variegated kinds in heavy shade – they will simply turn green.

Dryopteris filix-mas
H: 90cm (3ft)
The elegant light green semi-evergreen fronds of this fern unroll in spring. Unlike most ferns, it will cope with very dry shade.

Elaeagnus pungens
H: 3m (10ft)
Evergreen, bushy shrub with very fragrant small white flowers in autumn.

Epimedium sp.
This genus prefers moist shade, but will cope with dry shade if needs be. *E. grandiflorum* 'White Queen' has elegant heart-shaped leaves and large white flowers.

Euphorbia robbiae
H: 60cm (3ft) plus
This euphorbia will cope with dry shade, and makes excellent weed-suppressing evergreen ground cover. The large limy-green flowers last from spring until late summer.

Geranium sp.
There are so many of them that only a couple of preferences can be described. The white hybrids always seem to go well with other plants. *G. macrorrhizum album* is a little charmer, and also has sweet-scented leaves. *G. phaeum album* is a good shade plant.

Hedera sp.
There are literally hundreds of different forms of ivy, but one of the most elegant, for my money, is *H. helix* 'Sagittifolia', which has arrow-shaped leaves. *H. helix* 'Poetica Arborea' makes a dome-shaped bush that is covered with fruit that turn orange in spring. The king of ivies, for my money, is *H. colchica* 'Sulphur Heart' with its flamboyant large, heart-shaped leaves.

139

Ivy can also be trained successfully into imitation topiary shapes, which may well suit the style of a formal alleyway, and since it climbs over almost anything in its path, you are not limited to the floor of the garden.

Another splendid shade plant is the fern, although some do not like dry shade, and some do not like it damp. *Dryopteris filix-mas*, the buckler fern, will tolerate almost any situation except water-logged soil, and has wonderfully elegant fronds that deepen in colour during the season. It is not a true evergreen, but it nevertheless lasts well for most of the winter. Another tolerant fern is *Phyllitis scolopendrium*, the hart's tongue fern, which will put up with most conditions, although it does not like drought. It has a cluster of ribbon-like leaves. For damper soil, *Polypodium vulgare* makes good colonizing ground cover, and there are lots of varieties to choose from, such as 'Cornubiense' which has lighter green, more airy looking fronds than the species. For dense shade, try *Polystichum setiferum*.

Helleborus corsicus
H: 60cm (2ft) plus
The leaves are a wonderfully thick, glossy green, and the large heads of pale green, cup-shaped, drooping flowers appear in spring.

Hydrangea macro-phylla 'Bluebird'
H: 1.2m (4ft)
Deciduous bushy shrub with flat open mauvy blue heads of flowers. Leaves turn red in autumn. *H. quercifolia* is a little bigger, with unusual deeply lobed leaves that turn good colours in autumn.

Polypodium vulgare
H: 30cm (12in)
A good evergreen fern for ground cover in fairly damp soil, it comes in many forms. *P.v.* 'Cornubiense' is a prettier form, with lighter green, more delicate fronds.

Polystichum setiferum 'Plumosa'
H: 60cm (2ft)
A velvety evergreen or semi-evergreen fern for dense shade, it looks very good planted with hostas and pulmonarias.

Rheum palmatum
H: 2m (6ft)
This ornamental rhubarb does well in shady situations, producing huge hand-shaped leaves from its crowns. Makes a wide spreading plant, with every few years, a magnificent, 2.3m- (8ft-) tall flower spike. Needs lots of organic matter in the soil and plenty of moisture to do well.

Rhododendron 'Loderi'
H: 4m (13ft)
Huge clusters of fragrant, trumpet-shaped flowers are borne in spring, in shades of pink to white.

R. yakushimanum
H and S: 1.2m (4ft)
Evergreen, attractively dome-shaped rhododendron with pink flowers in late spring, that gradually fade to white.

Skimmia japonica 'Rubella'
H: 1.5m (5ft)
Evergreen, upright shrub with aromatic bright green foliage and pinky red flower buds in winter.

Trachystemon orientalis
H: 30cm (12in)
The king of large-leaved plants for dry shade, it is a good, tough, stand-by as ground cover. It has blue, rather insignificant flowers in spring.

OPPOSITE, TOP The large leaves are *Acanthus mollis*; the mossy plant is *Soleirolia soleirolii*.
OPPOSITE, BOTTOM A large pot by Monica Young, surrounded by *Ligularia dentata* 'Desdemona' on the right, *Trachystemon orientalis* behind and *Symphytum grandiflorum* in front.
LEFT The hosta in the foreground is *H. ventricosa* 'Aureo-maculata'; at the back is *H.* 'Frances Williams'.

Plants for sun

With its dark green finely cut leaves that last well for much of the year, *A. spinosus* flowers more freely in full sun, bearing greenish-purple hooded flowers on tall spires.

Agapanthus campanulatus
H: 1m (3ft)
Clumps of strap-shaped leaves surround the stems of brilliant blue flowers in late summer. It will grow almost any-where in warm climates.

Allium christophii
H: 75cm (2ft 6in)
Summer-flowering bulb with strappy leaves and huge starry flower heads in pale mauve. Looks good planted with thistles.

Alstroemeria ligtu hybrids
H: 60cm (2ft)
Summer-flowering tuber with freckled pink, yellow or bronze flowers. Does not like to be disturbed.

Asphodeline lutea
H: 1.2m (4ft)
The yellow asphodel has thick spikes of starry yellow flowers in spring.

Chrysanthemum frutescens
H: 1m (3ft)
Pure-white marguerites with golden eyes in mid-summer. They look very good planted in con-tainers.

Cynara cardunculus
H: 2m (6ft)
The cardoon is a splendid foliage plant, with huge arching silvery leaves and electric blue thistle heads of flowers. Sets off blue and mauve flowering plants to perfection.

Silvery, much divided foliage and strong flower colours epitomize plants that thrive in full sun, many of them being natives to the Mediterranean regions. They generally enjoy dry soil and will therefore normally withstand periods of drought.

IF YOU ARE fortunate enough to live in a warm and sunny climate, or indeed if a part of your garden is sheltered from wind and exposed to full sun, you will find that you can grow the plants that thrive in what is called a Mediterranean climate – in other words where there is plenty of sun. You will find that not only is the amount of sunshine crucial to the kinds of plants you can grow, but so is the amount of rainfall. Plants that like warmth and dampness are not the same as those that like it warm and dry, so you need to know the prevailing conditions.

If you have a south-facing bed, for example, which is backed by a wall, the conditions will be a lot drier than if the bed was in the open, as the wall provides shelter from the rain. It will also make the bed much hotter, reflecting back the sun's rays on to the plants below. In these conditions, you can

grow some of the very special, rather tender climbers, such as the trumpet vine (*Campsis radicans*) with its festoons of exotic-looking trumpet-shaped flowers, the passion flower (*Passiflora caerulea*), *Jasminum officinale*, with its scented white flowers, and the pretty white-flowered *Solanum jasminoides* 'Album'.

Among the good wall shrubs, as opposed to climbers, for these warm, dry conditions are the evergreen, scented, white *Carpenteria californica*, *Cytisus battandieri*, with its yellow, pineapple-scented flowers, and the massive *Magnolia grandiflora*, if your wall is big enough. One of the most worthwhile wall shrubs, although it does need a well-protected position, is *Fremontodendron californicum*. This shrub is hardier than it looks and will produce its

Echinops ritro
H: 1.2m (4ft)
Another worthwhile this-tle, with deeply cut silvery foliage and roundish heads of blue flowers.

Eryngium giganteum
H: 1.8m (6ft)
This makes a good back of the border plant, with its silvery-green thistle heads and attractive steely foliage.

Felicia amelloides 'Santa Anita'
H: 30cm (12in)
Evergreen sub-shrub with bright blue daisy-like flowers over a long flowering season, from late spring to autumn.

Fremontodendron californicum
H: 6m (20ft)
Evergreen shrub that needs protection. Beautiful, saucer-shaped golden flowers are borne from late spring to autumn. Needs full sun and well-drained soil.

Fritillaria imperialis
H: 1.5m (5ft)
Majestic spring-flowering bulb with heads of drooping orange bells. *F.i.* 'Lutea' is a cultivar with yellow flowers.

Galtonia candicans
H: 1.2m (4ft)
The summer hyacinth, which hails from South Africa, is a tall, elegant plant with a spire of drooping white bells in summer. Like most bulbous plants, it needs free-draining soil.

ABOVE The Chinese lantern lily (*Sandersonia auranti-aca*) with *Achillea* 'Moonshine' behind.
LEFT *Phlomis fruticosa* with *Sisyrinchium striatum* in front.
OPPOSITE Massed planting of *Verbena bonariensis*.

143

Lavandula sp.

There are many forms of lavender, some tall, some dwarf, some rich deep purple, some pale lilac, all of them deliciously scented. The French lavender, *L. stoechas*, with its densely packed spires of rich purple flowers, growing to about 1m (3ft), is one of the best, as is *L. angustifolia* 'Munstead', again with deep purple flower spikes.

Magnolia grandiflora

H: 10m (32ft)
The large oblong evergreen leaves make a good backdrop for the magnificent big white flowers from summer to autumn. *M.g.* 'Exmouth' is a good cultivar.

Onopordum acanthium

H: 2m (6ft) plus
This giant thistle is great for wild gardens or as a background for alliums and galtonias. Let it seed and spread itself around.

Osteospermum 'Whirlygig'

H: 60cm (2ft)
Evergreen perennial with bluish-white unusually shaped open, fringed, flowers in summer.

Passiflora caerulea

H: 10m (32ft)
This evergreen climber is fast-growing in full sun. It has exquisite purple- and green-flushed white flowers in summer, followed by passion fruits, given the right climate and conditions.

TOP *Eryngium giganteum*. RIGHT The purple spikes of *Acanthus spinosus* with *Miscanthus sacchariflorus*. FAR RIGHT The white heads of *Agapanthus africanus* 'Alba' above *Lavandula stoechas*.

144

large golden rose-type flowers, set against greeny-grey foliage, for most of the summer. Make sure it has good drainage, and that its roots do not get waterlogged in winter. *Fremontodendron* looks good combined with euphorbias and *Carpenteria*.

Many of the succulents needs warm, dry conditions, rewarding you with splendidly exotic, spiky foliage. Agaves, yuccas and phormiums are among some of the best. Other exotic-looking plants for the dry sunny garden are the crown imperials, *Fritillaria imperialis*, with their tall spires of down-turned bells and *Galtonia candicans* with its head of drooping white bells. *Agapanthus* is a tough, easy-to-grow, and equally impressive tall perennial for sunny situations, with its electric blue flowers. Most of the thistle family do well in hot sun, including *Onopordum acanthium*, a massive member of the family with huge rosettes of spiny leaves covered in felted, white down, and a flowering stem of pale lilac flowers. Its kissing cousin, *Cynara cardunculus*, also makes a massive column of grey foliage, covered with blue thistle flowers in summer.

Over the centuries plants have adapted to conditions, and sometimes a closer look at leaf forms will give you a clue as to the plants needs. Silvery, grey-felted, hairy and finely dissected leaves are adaptations that nature has provided for coping with hot, dry conditions. Stachys, cinerarias and senecios are among these.

Many of the daisies do particularly well in dry sunny borders, and make wonderful subjects for massed plantings in containers, where their sprawling mass is successfully restrained.

ABOVE *Geranium psilostemon* mixed with *Lychnis coronaria*.

ABOVE LEFT Mixed planting of scented herbs including borage, *Salvia turkestanica*, thymes, feverfew, *Monarda* and *Santolina virens*.

Sisyrinchium striatum
H: 60cm (2ft)
Useful spiky foliaged semi-evergreen plant, with variegated cream-striped leaves, and spikes of purple-striped yellow flowers in summer.

Stipa gigantea
H: 2m (6ft)
Arching clumps of neat, narrow green leaves with oatlike flower heads in gold and bronze.

Verbena bonariensis (syn. V. patagonica)
H: 1.5m (5ft)
From a basal clump of leaves arise tall flowering stems bearing florets of tiny purple flowers in summer.

145

Exotic plants

Agave americana
H: 1.5m (5ft)
Striking spiny-edged
sword-shaped leaves
grow in a large rosette.
A.a. 'Mediopicta' has
cream and green striped
leaves. Minimum temper-
ature: 4℃ (40℉).

Alocasia sp.
Good foliage plants with
arrow-shaped evergreen
leaves. *A macrorrhiza*
has leaves 1m (3ft) long.
Minimum temperature:
7℃ (40℉).

Bougainvillea glabra
H: Up to 10m (35ft) plus
Bougainvilleas come in
many colours, from the
rosy-purple of the species
through orange, yellow
and white forms.
Minimum temperature:
7℃ (45℉).

Bromeliads
There are several good
bromeliads with rosetted
leaves and showy flow-
ers. Try *Aechmea fasciata*
with big blue-grey leaves
and pink flowers and var-
ious guzmanias with
orange or yellow flowers.

Brugmansia suaveo-
lens (formerly *Datura*)
H: 1.8m (6ft) in container
Grown for its huge white
trumpet-shaped flowers,
which are heavily scent-
ed. Minimum tempera-
ture: 4℃ (40℉).

Caladium x *hortulanum*
Tuberous perennials with
showy, ornamental
leaves. Need partial
shade. Minimum temper-
ature: 18℃ (64℉).

ABOVE RIGHT *Gloriosa*
'Rothschildiana'
RIGHT Bromeliads, includ-
ing *Aechmea* and
Guzmania.

If you live in a warm climate, or have a con-
servatory that is heated in winter, you can
grow some of the tender and sub-tropical
plants that have a decidedly exotic appear-
ance, often with large, brilliantly coloured
flowers and lush evergreen foliage.

IF YOU LIVE in a warm climate, or if you have a conservatory in a colder one, you can grow some
wonderfully exotic-looking plants, with big leaves
and striking flowers. Tropical plants, by and large,
simply grow faster, look more lush and are more
colourful than plants from temperate areas of the
world, because the combination of light, heat and
moisture increases their growth rate.

Nurseries and garden centres are gradually
increasing their range of exotic plants, and nowadays you can find a good selection to choose from,
among them palms, banana plants, with their massive, handsome leaves, cannas, philodendrons,
bromeliads (which are epiphytical – in other words
they grow on other plants), orchids and many more.
It would be impossible to give more than a taste in
this book of the myriad tropical plants.

Because the plants grow quickly, you need to think through any design combinations carefully. The plants are often in flower, spectacular though these may be, for only short periods of time – orchids, bromeliads and cannas among them – and they are therefore best grown in pots, so that they can be moved to less prominent positions when they are not in flower.

Climbers play a valuable part in any planting scheme, and among the best are *Thunbergia grandiflora* with its pale blue flowers and the rampant *Bougainvillea glabra*, with its purply red bracts that appear in great profusion.

Orchids and ferns look good in hanging baskets, suspended from some kind of pergola or frame, and in pots on the ground you can grow heliconias, cannas and large bird's nest ferns (*Asplenium nidus*)

along with cycads and other small palms in pots. Bromeliads are a wonderful choice for a tropical effect, as they can be grown in baskets or attached to the branches of other woody-stemmed plants. Their brightly coloured foliage and sensual-looking flowers never fail to please and many of them quickly reproduce themselves, making little 'pups' next to the parent plant. I have a weakness for tree ferns – *Dicksonia fibrosa* for example – and these, too, look good grown in large pots. Their strong structural shapes make a cool background for brightly flowering plants, like hibiscus and oleanders.

Aim for a good balance between foliage and flowering plants, and try to ensure that the planting display is on more than one level. Be prepared to move pots around to give different plants exposure to sunlight.

Cycas revoluta
H: 3m (10ft)
Has a stout trunk topped with typical palm fronds. Minimum temperature: 13°C (55°F).

Ensete ventricosum
H: 6m (20ft)
This banana plant has huge, heavily ribbed evergreen leaves carried in a rosette. Frost-tender.

***Gloriosa* 'Rothschildiana'**
H: 2m (6ft)
The summer-flowering glory lily climbs using tendrils. Minimum temperature: 18°C (64°).

Peperomia caperata
H: 15cm (6in)
Bushy little evergreen foliage plant with fleshy leaves. Minimum temperature: 10°C (50°F).

Philodendron domesticum
H: 3m (10ft)
This evergreen clinging climber has large arrow-shaped leaves. Minimum temperature: 15°C (60°F).

Plumeria rubra
H: 4m (13ft)
Deciduous shrub with fragrant white flowers and handsome large leaves. Minimum temperature: 13°C (55°F).

LEFT The arrow-shaped leaves of *Caladium*, with *Peperomia* below them. BELOW *Cycas revoluta*.

Architectural plants

Arundo donax
H: 2.5m (8-9ft)
This broad-leaved grass
also comes in a variegat-
ed form, *A.d.* 'Versicolor'
with creamy white, verti-
cally striped leaves.

***Cardiocrinum
giganteum***
H: 1.8m (6ft) plus
A massive lily, this
has strap-shaped leaves
and spectacular long
trumpet-shaped creamy-
coloured flowers,
streaked with red inside,
that are also fragrant. It
needs moist, humus-rich
soil in partial shade.

Choisya ternata
H: 1.8m (6ft)
The Mexican orange blos-
som is a particularly good
evergreen shrub with att-
ractive whorls of bright,
glossy, green leaves
and clusters of fragrant
white flowers in spring.

Cordyline australis
H: 3m (10ft) in container,
up to 15m (50ft) in native
habitat. Produces a star-
burst of slender, spiky
leaves on a slender trunk.
Not totally hardy.

Crambe cordifolia
H: 2m (6ft)
Easy-to-grow perennial
with handsome, crinkled,
lobed leaves and clouds
of starry white flowers in
summer that rise above
the leaves.

RIGHT *Onopordum
acanthium*, with wisteria
above, and *Choisya
ternata*.
FAR RIGHT The giant
hogweed (*Heracleum
mantegazzianum*) with
Polygonum bistorta below.
OPPOSITE An ornamental
grape vine (*Vitis* sp.) with
Lavandula 'Hidcote'.

Any good planting scheme must have some feature plants to which the eye is automatically drawn. Thistles, ferns and grasses are among some of the best of these, and, in general, those with good foliage and/or form are the best for this purpose.

IT IS VERY EASY to be seduced by brilliant flower colour, but in terms of garden design the key to any good planting scheme lies in the form and texture of the plants as much as the colour – in other words their overall outline, leaf shapes and sizes, and the matt, glossy or reflective qualities of the foliage. You need to think carefully about the plants you choose for a small garden because, in fact, the one thing you should not do is 'think small' in terms of plant size, simply because the garden is small itself.

Ah, I hear you say, but if I use large plants, then I cannot have that many. True, but the handsome architectural plants you do include will repay you many times over for your self-restraint, because they will actually make the garden look larger and more restful, and add impact and interesting form to your planting scheme. Nothing is as tiresome, or as disturbing to the eye, as a planting scheme that is composed almost entirely of lots of small plants all jostling with each other gfor attention.

There are many good-shaped plants to suit every type of situation: dry, shallow soil, moist and warm conditions and, of course, wet and damp ones. You should try to think of your plants as pieces of living sculpture, and arrange them for their contrasting shapes in relation to each other. In other words, plant a tall grass like *Miscanthus*, with its long slender spiky leaves, next to a spreading large-leaved plant like *Fatsia*. Always try to plant in groups of odd numbers – in threes, fives or sevens – as it makes the outline of the group less rigid and formal. Not only is the selection of these larger, more architectural plants important, so is their positioning in the overall scheme. It is equally important to try and create interesting contrasts of form and texture, in foliage terms, between the plants themselves. As you quickly discover, foliage is not all one colour! Green can take many different hues from almost grey to almost yellow, and foliage comes in many other colours too – from purple to silver. Foliage has the double advantage that it is there for at least half of the year, and in terms of evergreens, it is a permanent feature in the garden, adding to the structural framework.

**Euphorbia
characias wulfenii**
H: 1.2m (4ft)
This evergreen shrub
makes large sprawling
mounds of bottlebrush-
like foliage with dense
heads of lime-green
flowers in spring.

x Fatshedera lizei
H: 2.2m (8ft)
This tree ivy has
attractive, deeply lobed,
glossy evergreen leaves,
with small white flowers
in autumn. It makes a
good mound shape. It
prefers sun.

Fatsia japonica
H and S: 3m (10ft)
One of the most effective
evergreen foliage plants
with its glossy dark green
leaves, it also makes a
neat, mound-shaped
bush. Produces tiny white
flowers in autumn, fol-
lowed by black fruits.

**Heracleum
mantegazzianum**
H: 2m (6ft) plus
This big perennial nor-
mally grows on the edge
of woodland, and it is
aggressive in many ways
– the sap is poisonous –
but it makes a striking
spire of a plant with large
leaves. Grow it if you dare!

**Hosta sieboldiana
'Elegans'**
H: 1m (3ft) plus
Huge bluish-grey thickly
ribbed leaves are the
hallmark of this particu-
larly elegant hosta. It
does best in partial shade.

Macleaya cordata
H: 2m (6ft)
This exotic looking blue-
grey leaved perennial,
with pinkish stems,
spreads very rapidly to
produce an entire thicket.
Clouds of small pinkish
flowers in summer.

RIGHT *Macleaya cordata*
behind with *Iris sibirica*
and *Matteuccia
struthiopteris*.

Ideally, you should aim for a balance between deciduous and evergreen plants in the garden, siting the evergreens at key points where you need a permanent focal point. There are a few really good evergreens with interesting leaves and good plant outlines, but they are less numerous than the deciduous plants.

Among the bold architectural evergreens that I use most frequently are *Choisya ternata*, with its neat, glossy, whorls of dark green leaves, *Fatsia japonica* with its large hand-shaped leaves, the bamboo, *Sasa palmata,* and *Elaeagnus pungens* for its background of silvery-grey foliage. *Rhododendron sinogrande* is an excellent large-leaved shrub, as is *Magnolia grandiflora* for a warm wall, and *Viburnum davidii* for lower-level ground cover. The fan palm, *Trachycarpus fortunei*, is another good feature plant but requires careful positioning so as not to look out of context with the surrounding foliage.

There are also lots of big perennials that are worthy of including in most gardens, some of which are discussed in other sections. *Rheum palmatum*, the

ornamental rhubarb, is a truly magnificent plant with its generous maple-shaped leaves and dark red stems (see also page 141).

Other perennial favourites are hostas, with their thick, ribbed leaves and attractive urn-shaped mound of foliage. *Hosta sieboldiana* 'Elegans' is an unfailingly good choice. *Macleaya cordata* is another good stand-by, making a thick screen of attractive grey-green leaves, standing nearly 2m (6ft) tall. Among other splendid performers are thistles, ferns and grasses, all discussed in more detail on pages 132-7.

Climbing plants with large leaves also make a strong architectural impact, particularly the large-leaved ornamental vine (*Vitis coignetiae*) and the Dutchman's pipe (*Aristolochia macrophylla*). Climbers tend to be considered as largely flowering plants, such as clematis and roses, but those with strong, bold foliage are excellent for clothing pergolas and I, for one, find the foliage of wisteria as attractive as the flowers.

Don't forget the plants with strappy or sword-shaped leaves – the yuccas, cordylines and even irises – which help to make a punctuation point amongst more rounded foliage forms. In more sheltered gardens, you could include the tree fern (*Dicksonia antarctica*). If you grow it in a container, you can bring it under cover in winter. Its fern-like foliage on top of a stout trunk creates an excellent focal point. Alternatively, use the palm, *Chamaerops humilis*, in the same way.

Miscanthus sinensis **'Zebrinus'**
H: 1.2m (4ft)
Graceful, like all the grasses, this one makes an attractive clump of variegated leaves with white ring markings.

Verbascum bombyciferum
H: 1.4m (5ft)
Soldier-like biennial with tall spires of yellow flowers in summer, and softly felted silvery grey leaves.

Vitis coignetiae
H: 15m (50ft)
A vigorous ornamental vine with large leaves that turn an attractive reddish-bronze in autumn.

Yucca gloriosa
H: To 1.2m (4ft)
Known also as the Spanish dagger, this has a crown of narrow, sword-shaped evergreen leaves on a stout stem.

LEFT *Hosta sieboldiana* 'Elegans' with *Iris sibirica* 'Alba'.
BELOW *Cynara cardunculus*, with clipped box balls.

151

Screening plants

Hedges, boundaries, balconies and walls all need plants that will provide both shelter and privacy. There is a wide range of trees, climbers and shrubs for different situations and purposes.

THE PLANTS that clothe the walls and fences in the garden, or create their own green tapestry as a boundary, as well as those that divide one part of the garden from another are key players in the design of small spaces. If you take a look at any garden that has no vertical screening elements you are immediately struck both by the total lack of privacy and the feeling of unease induced by it. For a small garden to work well, you have to pay attention to its boundaries, for no other reason, often, than that neighbouring buildings or unsightly objects intrude on your view.

Screening plants can be divided into categories of height as well as type. There are those suitable for blocking off unattractive views, such as trees, those that provide a dense and impenetrable barrier at a lower level, such as hedging plants and grasses, and those that cover existing structures, providing colour, interest and protection, such as climbing or scrambling plants.

Trees

The taller plants – the trees – have to be chosen with great care in a small garden, because if they are too tall, or too spreading, you will severely restrict what you can grow underneath them. Since there is a shortage of space anyway, the tree has to work hard for its keep, and ideally should provide you with a rewarding picture in several seasons – attractive foliage in spring, flowers and/or fruit in summer, and good autumn colour in winter. Flowering crab apples and hawthorns are valuable in this respect. Trees with attractive bark, like silver birches, as well as attractive shape are also good subjects for the smaller garden. Alternatively, if the plant is an evergreen, it provides a permanent structural feature in the garden, although too many evergreens in a small garden can create a very dense, solid feel to it. The most interesting gardens contain a mixture of evergreens and deciduous trees and shrubs.

Growing trees is, to me, rather like raising children: every year they grow a bit bigger, and every year they demand a bit more space; on top of that, you have to clean up after them regularly. But for all their faults, trees do provide the essential backbone to the planting.

The first and foremost consideration when planting a tree is the size that it will eventually make. Some trees are surprisingly fast growing and, in a very short space of time, their branches may intrude into neighbouring gardens or their roots cause havoc by lifting up paving or cracking walls. Do seek advice from a reputable nurseryman on the habit of any tree that you consider buying. Among some of the best small trees are catalpas, paulownia and cleredendrum. The yellow-leaved *Catalpa bignoniodes* does not get much beyond 3m (10ft)

Trees for small gardens

Aralia elata
Arbutus andrachne
A. unedo
Betula utilis
Carpinus cordata
Crataegus oxyacantha
'Paul's Double Scarlet'
C. prunifolia
Eucryphia nymansensis
Gleditsia triacanthos
'Sunburst'
Hippophae rhamnoides
Hoheria populnea
Idesia polycarpa
Ilex sp.
Laburnum alpinum
L. vossii
Magnolia sp.
Malus sp.
Paulownia tomentosa
Populus tremula
Prunus sp. (many forms)

Quick-growing trees with large leaves

Catalpa sp.
Clerodendrum fargesii
Paulownia sp.
Populus lasiocarpa

Small evergreen trees

Arbutus x *andrachnoides*
A. menziesii
A. unedo
Castanopsis chrysophylla
C. cuspidata
Eucalyptus gunnii
Ilex aquifolium
Laurus nobilis
Magnolia grandiflora
Nothofagus betuloides
Quercus coccifera
Taxus baccata

RIGHT *Gleditsia triacanthos* 'Sunburst'.
FAR RIGHT *Catalpa speciosa* grown as standards.

in height and is an excellent subject for a small garden. *Paulownia tomentosa* has wonderfully scented foxglove-type flowers in early summer and *Clerodendrum bungei* is also scented.

Another of my favourites is *Eriobotrya japonica*, the loquat, which is a handsome evergreen with large, leathery leaves. I have never managed to get it to fruit in the British Isles, but I can remember as a small boy spending hours climbing this tree in New Zealand to get at the fruit.

There is nothing stopping you from growing trees in large containers. The Japanese maples (*Acer palmatum*) are excellent subjects for this, as are hollies (*Ilex* sp.), the strawberry tree (*Arbutus unedo*) and the Japanese cedar (*Cryptomeria japonica*). *Pittosporum tobira* has wonderfully scented summer flowers smelling like orange blossom.

Carefully chosen trees and shrubs provide excellent shelter and protection and offer a great deal more visually than a straight line of walling or fencing, particularly if the trees and shrubs are varied, and also staggered when planted.

Climbers

Climbers of many sorts are very useful screening plants, attached either to walls or fences, or to trellises and pergolas. Those with thick, evergreen foliage, such as ivy, can mask unattractive boundary walls, while those with more delicate foliage and attractive flowers will look good festooned over arches, pergolas or trellis to divide one part of the garden from another or, on a roof terrace, to provide some kind of windbreak. A mixture can sometimes be the best solution, with some large-leaved, ornamental vines, such as *Vitis coignetiae*, or virginia creeper, perhaps, mingled with more attractive

ABOVE Different varieties of the Japanese maple (*Acer palmatum dissectum*) grown in pots.
LEFT *Michelia doltsopa* grown as topiary. In temperate climates, the same effect could be achieved with clipped privet or yew.

Trees with dense shape
Aeculus sp.
Albizia julibrissin
Carpinus sp.
Crataegus sp.
Ficus sp.
Gleditsia triacanthos
Malus sp.
Prunus sp.
Robinia pseudoacacia
Sophora sp.
Sorbus sp.

153

flowering climbers like jasmine, honeysuckle, clematis or roses.

Many of the climbing plants and wall shrubs are also highly perfumed, in particular many roses, most honeysuckles, wisteria, jasmines, *Carpenteria californica*, *Clematis flammula* (which smells of almonds), *Magnolia grandiflora*, *Trachelospermum jasminoides* and *Chimonanthus praecox* to name but a few of them.

There is a wonderful range of both climbers and wall-shrubs to choose from, some of which I have listed in the appropriate sections on sun and shade.

In a small garden, it pays to grow one climber over another to get the most out of the space, and prolong the flowering season. Roses and clematis are ideal plants for this treatment, and if you choose them with care, you can achieve some wonderful combinations of scent and colour. People often think of clematis as summer-flowering plants, but there are so many of them that you can find a clematis that starts flowering in early spring, and one that flowers in late autumn, and others to fill all the months in between.

Hedges and low screens

Dividing the garden into compartments can be done successfully with a variety of hedging plants that are clipped to keep them to the right size and scale:

evergreen box, yew and privet for permanent formal screening; and deciduous beech and hornbeam for softer divisions of larger spaces.

Partial seasonal as well as permanent screens can be provided by grasses and bamboos, and by using evergreen shrubs at certain punctuation points in the design, to add perspective to it and prevent the observer from taking in the whole garden at a glance.

Plants for shelter

Screening plants are essential if your garden is exposed in any way – particularly if you have a roof terrace or balcony. There are some particularly good plants which act as a shelter belt from the wind. Evergreens are clearly among the best contenders as their year-round foliage provides constant protection. Among them are the tough leathery leaved hollies (*Ilex* sp.), some of which have attractively variegated leaves, pyracantha, with its brilliant coloured berries, in red, orange or yellow, and elaeagnus, with little, very fragrant flowers in autumn. *Elaeagnus pungens* makes good, strong, evergreen, hedging.

If you live near the sea, you need screening plants that will tolerate exposure to both wind and salt-spray. Among some of the best for these conditions are *Euonymus*, *Griselinia* and *Ceanothus*.

Climbers for trellis, walls, fences
Actinidia kolomikta
Akebia quinata
Bougainvillea glabra
Campsis radicans
Clematis sp. (many cultivars and hybrids)
Fremontodendron californicum
Hedera sp.
Jasminum sp.
Lonicera sp.
Mandevilla laxa
Parthenocissus henryana
Polygonatum sp.
Rosa sp. (many)
Solanum jasminoides
Trachelospermum jasminoides
Vitis coignetiae
Wisteria sinensis

OPPOSITE *Clematis* 'Etoile Violette' grown with *Rosa* 'Bantry Bay'.
FAR LEFT *Clematis* 'Prince Charles' grown with *Rosa* 'Pink Clouds'.
LEFT *Wisteria sinensis* grown over an arch with clipped box balls underneath.

Griselinia littoralis, which hails from my native New Zealand, is on the tender side, but makes an excellent coastal area screening plant in slightly warmer climates. *Pittosporum tobira*, with its fragrant creamy flowers, is another good evergreen subject for coastal areas. *Hippophae rhamnoides*, the sea buckthorn, is a tougher customer with its spiny, silvery leaves. If you grow male and female plants together, you will get bright orange berries in autumn and winter. To make a dense hedge, plant young plants about 45cm (18in) apart, and then trim off the upper third of the shoots to encourage bushiness.

Once you have created a reasonably solid screen of hedging plants, you can use the protection they provide to grow some more interesting, and rather more delicate plants, in its lee.

Unusual climbers
Aristolochia durior
Campsis x *tagliabuana*
'Mme Galen'
Clematis armandii
Eccremocarpus scaber
Hardenbergia
comptoniana
Ipomea sp.
Lapageria rosaea
Lathyrus odorata
Rhodochiton sp.
Runner beans
(*Phaeseolus* sp.)
Thunbergia alata

Evergreen shrubs for roof gardens
Buxus sp.
Ceanothus sp.
Cistus sp.
Cotoneaster sp.
Elaeagnus pungens
Griselinia sp.
Ilex sp.
Laurus nobilis
Lonicera x
hildebrandiana
Mahonia x *media*
'Charity'
Myrtus communis
Osmanthus delavayi
Pittosporum tobira
Prunus laurocerasus
Pyracantha sp.
Rosmarinus sp.
Viburnum davidii

TOP *Plumbago canadensis* with *Mandevilla laxa*. RIGHT Honeysuckle (*Lonicera* x *tellmaniana*) with ligularias.

Screening plants for compartments
Arundo donax
Bamboos (Sasa sp.)
Cordyline australis
Eriobotrya japonica
Fatsia japonica
Gunnera manicata
Kalmia sp.
Macleaya cordata
Miscanthus sinensis
Nandina domestica
Phlomis fruticosa
Rhododendron sp.
Trachycarpus fortunei
Yucca gloriosa

TOP *Campsis* x *tagliabuana* 'Mme Galen'.
LEFT *Hydrangea petiolaris*.

Container plants

In theory, almost any plant can be grown in a container but the point of using containers is to focus attention on the planting, so it pays to be selective, choosing plants with good foliage and form attractive flowers.

THERE IS REALLY almost no limit to what you can grow in containers, except naturally very deep-rooted plants, which would rapidly outgrow the space available to them. Ideally, however, you need to choose plants that are eye-catching in either shape, foliage, form or colour, because the container focuses attention on the plants within it, and if these are not strong subjects in their own right, the impact is lost. For the same reason, it is extremely important to ensure that container plants are in good condition. Nothing looks worse than array of containers with drooping, diseased or dying plants.

The container must be large enough for the shape and form of the plant, and the texture and colour of the container should complement the plant material it contains. For example the bluish-grey-

Plants for form and foliage colour
Acer palmatum (and hybrids)
Aculea sp.
Agave sp.
Aloe sp.
Bamboos (*Sasa* sp.)
Chamaerops humilis
Cordyline australis
Dracaena sp.
Ferns, including tree ferns (*Dicksonia* sp.) and *Polystichum* sp.
Hosta sp.
Iris confusa
Ligularia sp.
Phoenix roebelii (and other *Phoenix* species)
Phormium sp.
Pittosporum sp.
Punicea granata
Trachycarpus fortunei
Washingtonia sp.
Yucca gloriosa (and other *Yucca* species)

For flowers
Acanthus sp.
Alocasia sp.
Agapanthus sp.
Campanula sp.
Canna sp.
Coreopsis sp.
Echeveria sp.
Euphorbia sp.
Helianthemum sp.
Helleborus sp.
Kalanchoe sp.
Nicotiana sp.
Salvia sp.
Saxifraga sp.
Solanum sp.
Tibouchina sp.
Verbascum sp.

leaved *Hosta sieboldiana* 'Elegans' looks very good in a dark blue ceramic pot. It is a good idea to have a mixture of plant types in containers, some small trees or shrubs, some perennials and some displays of bulbs and annuals that you change with the seasons, but I do not like to see a mixture in a container. It is better to restrict the planting to one type of plant for each pot.

Containers dry out extremely fast, and will need regular watering. Also, you will need to add plenty of nutrients to the compost to supplement those taken out by the plant and those removed by the constant watering that is required.

One of the benefits of containers is that you are able to grow plants that will not thrive in the normal

ABOVE *Hosta* 'Frances Williams' in the centre with *H.* 'Blue Moon' to the left and *H. sieboldiana* to the right.
LEFT Verbena hybrids, 'Derby Series', and purple sage.
FAR LEFT *Hydrangea macrophylla* with clipped box and standard fuchsias.

Bulbs
Allium sp.
Cyclamen sp.
Fritillaria sp.
Galtonia candicans
Hyacinthus sp.
Lilium sp.
Muscari sp.
Narcissus sp.
Tulipa sp.

climate of your area or the existing soil conditions in your garden. Provided you have somewhere to over-winter the plants, such as a conservatory, you can indulge your tastes with some of the tropical plants shown on pages 146-7, or equally you can use containers to grow plants, such as camellias or azaleas, that only thrive in acid soil. You can choose the soil type and make it specially to suit the types of plant – acid or chalky, sandy or peat, and so on.

Planting schemes in containers look better if kept simple. I prefer to plant up large containers of a single species for maximum impact, although occasionally it is worth including some plants with attractive foliage – such as hostas, zantedeschias or bamboos – to back up a display that concentrates on a single flower colour.

BELOW Mixed display of love-in-a-mist (*Nigella* sp.), *Cosmos* 'Sunny Red' and *Centaurea cyanus* 'Jubilee Gem'.
BELOW RIGHT Single colour theme of soft apricot using pansies (*Viola* sp.)

Climbers for pots
Actinidia kolomikta
Bougainvillea glabra
Campsis radicans
Clematis sp. (many)
Cobaea scandens
Eccremocarpus scaber
Hedera (most species)
Hydrangea petiolaris
Ipomea sp.
Jasminum officinale
Lonicera sp.
Mandevilla laxa
Passiflora caerulea
Solanum jasminoides
Thunbergia elata
*Trachelospermum
    jasminoides*
Vitis sp.
Wisteria sinensis

Annuals
Amaranthus sp.
Begonia sp.
Calendula sp.
Dahlia sp.
Gazania sp.
Impatiens sp.
Mesembryanthemum sp.
Nicotiana sp.
Osteospermum sp.
Pelargonium sp.
Portulacca sp.
Verbena sp.
Zinnia sp.

Herbs
Basil (*Ocimum basilicum*)
Chives (*Allium
    schoenoprasum*)
Garlic (*Allium sativum*)
Mint (*Mentha* sp.)
Parsley (*Petroselinum
    crispum*)
Rosemary
    (*Rosmarinus* sp.)
Sage (*Salvia* sp.)
Tarragon (*Artemisia* sp.)
Thyme (*Thymus* sp.)

TOP Pots of *Brachy-
scome iberidifolia* with
Alchemilla mollis and
Erigeron karvinskianus.
Pots by Chris Lewis.
FAR LEFT Ferns (*Dryopteris
filix-mas*) and pots in Ivan
Hicks' garden.
LEFT Dwarf variety of
*Chrysanthemum
frutescens* in a pot by
Chris Lewis.

161

Moisture-loving plants

5

Acorus calamus 'Variegatus'
H: 75cm (30in)
The sweet flag grows in the water's margins. Its handsome semi-evergreen strappy leaves are striped cream and green, and are tangerine scented.

Aponogeton distachyos
S: 1.2m (4ft)
This deep-water plant is a good substitute for water lilies in a more shady pond. It produces waxy white flowers from late spring to autumn.

RIGHT *Primula pulverulenta* with *Rodgersia podophylla* and *Iris sibirica*.
BELOW *Iris laevigata*.

Pools and bog gardens offer the opportunity to grow an interesting range of plants that tend to be both large and lush. There is usually room, even in a small garden, for a pool and it is worthwhile creating one just for the opportunity to grow some of these plants.

A SMALL WATER feature not only makes a splendid visual change of focus and a change of pace in the garden, it also provides the opportunity to grow some more unusual plants, particularly if you have a boggy margin to a natural pool, or you create its equivalent artificially with a butyl liner. Positioning the plants is crucial to the impact they will make. Try to clump them together in groups of species, rather than scattering them around the water feature like confetti, and make sure that you create some good contrasts of leaf shape and texture – using the sword-shaped leaves

of irises or the strappy leaves of rushes, perhaps, as a foil to the softer mounds of ligularias and hostas.

Most water plants have attractive foliage that stays looking fresh for a large part of the year. Among the more dramatic pool-side performers are *Gunnera manicata*, with its massive parasols of foliage up to 2m (6ft) or more broad, the bright green, almost circular, foliage of *Petasites japonicus*, albeit invasive, and many superb ligularias. The various water-loving iris, including the Japanese iris, *I. ensata* and *I. laevigata*, are all worth growing, as much for their handsome sword-shaped swathes of leaves as for their delicate-looking papery flowers. Quite a few of the more attractive waterside plants are also unfortunately rather invasive. *Lysichiton americanus* will bid to take over the space if given a chance, as indeed will the pretty blue-flowered *Pontederia cordata*. Tough action is needed to keep

Butomus umbellatus
H: 1.2m (4ft)
A rush-like marginal plant, it needs an open, sunny site and up to 25cm (10in) of water. Tall, slender leaves and umbels of pinky red flowers in summer.

Gunnera manicata
H: 2m (6ft) plus, and wide spreading
Massive though this plant is, do not be put off, even in a small garden. The leaves are probably the largest of any perennial, and are prickly edged. Light green flower spikes appear in early summer. It is slightly tender, and the crown needs to be protected in winter.

Houttuynia cordata
H: 30cm (12in)
Prefers moist soil or waterside conditions, and will make good ground cover although it can be invasive. *H.c.* 'Chamaeleon' has attractively variegated leaves that are heart-shaped, flushed with pink.

Iris ensata (syn. I. kaempferi)
H: 1m (3ft)
This beardless Japanese iris has the usual strap-shaped iris leaves and purplish flowers with a yellow stripe on the falls in summer. It prefers partial shade.

Iris pseudacorus
H: Up to 1.8m (6ft)
The yellow flag has golden flowers with brown veining from early summer. It needs semi-shade and thrives in very damp soil. The variegated form, *I.p.* 'Variegata', has yellow and green striped foliage.

FAR LEFT *Iris ensata*.
LEFT *Pontederia cordata* with *Miscanthus sinensis* 'Zebrinus'.

163

Iris sibirica
H: Up to 1.2m (4ft)
The Siberian flag, a beard-less iris, prefers boggy conditions. Up to 2 or 3 dark blue flowers per stem from late spring.

Ligularia dentata 'Desdemona'
H: 1.2m (4ft)
This will take full sun if grown in damp condi-tions, and also looks good in containers, with rich, moist soil. It has an unusual deep purple leaf colour, and seeds freely in ideal conditions.

Nymphaea 'Escarboule'
S: 3m (10ft)
Vigorous water lily with dark green leaves and cup-shaped deep red flowers, with golden stamens.

Peltiphyllum peltatum
H: 1.2m (4ft)
The umbrella plant, as it is sometimes called, is a spreading perennial with big rounded leaves. The clusters of pale pink flowers appear in spring before the leaves. It does best in boggy conditions in full sun.

Petasites japonicus
H: 60cm (2ft)
This handsome perennial has large, soft light green leaves that appear after the cones of yellowish-white flowers. It is, how-ever, very invasive. Will cope with partial shade.

Pontederia cordata
H: 75cm (30in)
The pickerel weed has glossy, dark green leaves and closely packed spikes of bright blue flowers in late summer. It grows in water, in the pond's mar-gins, and needs full sun.

RIGHT *Iris pseudacorus* 'Bastardii' with *Gunnera chilensis*, *Ligularia* 'The Rocket' and *Matteuccia struthiopteris*.

these plants in check, ruthlessly thinning them out whenever necessary.

For the water itself, water lilies (*Nymphaea* sp.) are a must, provided you have at least 1m (3ft) of still water, and plenty of sunshine on the pond itself. For a small garden, you are better off growing the smaller forms such as *N. pygmaea* 'Alba' with white flowers, and which can even be grown in a small tub. *N.* 'Escarboule' has larger flowers, in deep crimson, with dark foliage. Some of the water lilies are reputed to be scented, but as Christopher Lloyd pointed out in his book, *The Flower Garden*, it is not an easy theory to test.

If your pool is on the shady side, the water hawthorn (*Aponogeton distachyos*) is a good sub-stitute for water lilies with its long spires of waxy white flowers from spring to late autumn, and its elegant narrow leaves that fan out over the water.

Reeds and rushes make an excellent contrast of form and texture with more rounded leaf shapes. *Butomus umbellatus* is a handsome marginal reed with its umbrella-like flower heads.

If you are planning to stock your pond with fish, then you must include some oxygenating plants. You should do so anyway, as it will help keep the pond in good condition.

Primula sp.

The candelabra primula (*P. bulleyana*) grows to about 60cm (2ft) with deep orange flowers in early summer. The giant cowslip (*P. florindae*) has bright yellow flowers in summer while *P. pulverulenta* has deep red flowers with purplish red eyes in early summer.

Rodgersia sp.

These summer-flowering perennials make good water garden plants, and will grow in moist soil in sun or semi-shade. *R. pinnata* 'Superba', which grows to about 1.2m (4ft), has emerald green divided leaves and spires of pink flowers in summer.

Zantedeschia aethiopica

H: 1m (3ft)
Deep green leaves and arum-like white spathes in summer. It needs full sun but will grow in up to 30cm (12in) of water as a marginal plant. *Z.a.* 'Crowborough' has large, pure white spathes.

LEFT *Zantedeschia aethiopica* 'Crowborough'.
BELOW LEFT *Astilbe* 'Fanal' with low-growing thymes.
BELOW *Ligularia* 'The Rocket'.

There is a wide range of exciting elements that can be included when designing a garden, from gazebos, summer houses and pergolas to sculpture and ornaments, to give character and focus to the garden. This chapter takes a detailed look at some of the possibilities, with suggestions as to how they might be incorporated in the overall plan.

Effects & finishes

◆ LIGHTING ◆ FURNITURE ◆
◆ AL FRESCO EATING ◆
◆ SCULPTURE AND ORNAMENT ◆
◆ SWIMMING POOLS AND HOT TUBS ◆
◆ CONSERVATORIES ◆
◆ SUMMER HOUSES AND GAZEBOS ◆
◆ FANTASY AND FUN ◆

Lighting

For a small garden in a urban setting, it pays to make the maximum use of the space, so lighting at night is an important factor if you want to get the most from your garden. Lights add immeasurably to the atmosphere of the garden, transforming it into a place of mystery.

To MANY PEOPLE, lighting a garden may seem a rather ostentatious idea. And yet a few simple lights – such as flares on holders or candles – can make an almost magical transformation. Even mundane gardens take on an air of excitement and mystery when lit up, and it is really worth the relatively minor outlay on the equipment for the genuinely stunning effects you can achieve. In a small garden, you need little in the way of lighting – just two or three carefully positioned spotlights will probably suffice.

The aim is to create the light where it will have the most dramatic impact. Shining a spotlight up into a feature tree, for example, is extremely effective, as is lighting any water feature you may have in the garden. The latter are better lit from below, and today there is plenty of choice of waterproof light fittings for using in pools. Patios will certainly benefit from being illuminated by wall lights.

If you do not wish to go to the bother of installing a proper lighting circuit in the garden, you can, of course, use flares or candles, either instead of, or in addition to, any other lighting system. They both

Stage set

LEFT For atmosphere at night, there is nothing to beat candlelight. In this garden, their glow is reflected in the mirrors positioned on the wall behind. A downlighter, concealed in the eaves of the house, washes the patio below with a warm diffused glow. Lighting levels are as important as lighting positions, since the aim is to use enough light to create emphasis, but not so much that all the sense of theatre is lost.

Single subjects

LEFT Trees or large shrubs are ideal subjects to highlight as their branch formations catch the light. A tungsten or halogen uplighter is best positioned at the base of the tree or placed half way up the trunk to create interesting shadows. It is important, as in this case, to conceal the source of the light.

produce a wonderfully soft, romantic light that is ideal for the garden, but you will need shades for them if it is at all windy. Small ornamental lanterns are an excellent choice, because they shelter the light source and look good as well. Create small groups of lanterns and candles on a side table for an al fresco dinner party.

Lighting effects

The effects depend in part on the choice of lighting type. Directional spotlighting accentuates shapes and throws interesting shadows while downlighting through leaves and branches, for example, creates softened, dappled light. A combination of uplighters and downlighters creates the best results.

If you are designing a garden from scratch, it pays to incorporate a lighting plan into the overall scheme, so that you can plan the runs for the wires under any surfaces you intend to construct, which keeps them safely out of the way of spades or forks.

Practical considerations

Apart from visual appeal, another good reason for lighting your garden is for security purposes. It is an extremely effective burglar deterrent, since few intruders would wish to cross a well-lit area to try to break into the house. Lighting is also useful for your own personal safety at night, and a light over any entrance to the garden, on an automatic time switch, is well worthwhile installing. Steps, changes of level and paths can also be lit, marking your way more clearly. If the light sources are hidden, and the light diffused a little, it will make an attractive feature in its own right.

There are certain safety precautions you have to observe with any form of outdoor lighting, and most countries have their own regulations and specifications about thickness and insulation of cable, and so forth. Underwater lighting is an obvious example where waterproof fittings and fixings are essential, and these days it is possible to obtain quite a wide range of different types and styles of underwater light fittings.

The extent and style of the lighting scheme is a matter of personal choice, but surprisingly enough, small spaces sometimes require more lighting rather than less, particularly if the garden is used a lot for outdoor entertaining. Make sure any eating areas are well lit, with a choice of lighting intensity: dimmer switches are extremely useful. However, do not light up the area to the point where it resembles tinsel town, and make sure the lights are sufficiently spaced out to leave deep, mysterious pools of dark-

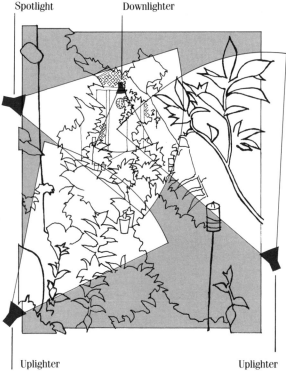

Spotlight   Downlighter

Uplighter   Uplighter

172

ness between the light sources, which not only produces a more natural feel but increases the feeling of spaciousness. The choice of styles of light fitting is almost infinite, but not all of them are attractive or suitable. Take care that those you choose blend in with the general theme and style of the garden. It is probably better to err on the side of neutrality, since it is the output of light that is important, rather than the fitting, which you cannot see once the lights are turned on. Ideally, therefore, you need light fittings that disappear into the planting during the day.

Lighting techniques

There are various different ways of creating visual impact with light, and the lighting professionals use different terms to describe the different effects.

Uplighting is used to illuminate a specific feature, such as a tree, and in this case the light source is positioned directly under the feature. *Moonlighting* creates a gentle glow by positioning the light source high up above the ground, usually in trees, to stimulate the diffuse and delicate light of the moon. You need to shield the light source in this position to avoid any glare. *Silhouette lighting* is used for subtle outline lighting, and is ideal if you wish to draw attention to a specific plant or ornament, and *spotlighting* is used to shine light directly onto a feature. *Mirror lighting* is used for underwater lighting, and is most effective with dark-bottomed pools and ponds of still water. If you light the planting on the opposite side of the pool from the viewer, you will produce wonderful reflections in the water itself.

Furniture

In small spaces, the furniture assumes a far greater importance than it would in a larger garden, and the style, design and function of the hard and soft furnishings becomes a major element in the planning of the garden style.

THE GARDEN FURNITURE is as important as the furniture for the house. Although you might conceivably get away with garden furniture that is not particularly special in a large country garden, where it fades into insignificance, given the scale of a small town garden, the furniture is much more noticeable, and a much more prominent feature.

Look for garden furniture that is well-designed, solid and durable. It will have to withstand everything that the weather can throw at it, so it has to be made to last. In very small gardens, it may be sensible to opt for folding chairs and tables, that can be stacked away, when you are not actually using them.

Most gardens benefit from having at least one permanent seat in a place for quiet contemplation. A small bench is probably the best choice in confined spaces, and there is a wide range today to choose from. It sometimes pays to paint or stain the bench a colour that blends in well with the planting, perhaps picking up a secondary colour scheme. Colours that almost always look good are a deep slatey blue, soft dark greens and silvery greys. White tends to stand out too sharply against cool, grey skies.

Size is another element to bear in mind. If you are planning to eat in the garden, you need to allow room to pull chairs back, and to walk around the furniture. In very small spaces, benches or built-in furniture may be better, with perhaps some

Chunky chairs

LEFT This folding chair, made from African hardwood, is not only comfortable, but practical for storing in winter and chunky enough to be solid and durable.

Spreading shade

LEFT Large umbrellas not only provide much-needed shade but are a decorative element in their own right. Being large, they must be well-secured at the base.

Gothic glory

OPPOSITE Furniture can be used as much as an ornament as for practical purposes. Well-designed or antique seats, for example, look good as a feature. This ancient gothic bench blends beautifully with the majestic spikes of *Acanthus mollis* behind.

cupboard space for garden equipment incorporated. Seats or tables built around tree bases can look extremely attractive and take up very little space.

Wooden furniture

For my money, wood is probably the most attractive material for furniture because it blends with almost any style, and it is also extremely versatile. If it is well made and solid, it will also be heavy, and if you want to be able to move the furniture around easily, then lighter metal furniture might be a better solution. Wood looks good in a natural finish, or you can paint or varnish it in a myriad of different ways, ringing the changes over the years if you wish. Some of the recently rediscovered paint distressing finishes look very good on garden furniture, enabling you to create in hours the kind of weathered, time-worn charm that it once took years to acquire.

All wooden furniture for outdoor use must be made of one of the hardwoods, such as teak, oak or elm, or one of the slightly less expensive African hardwoods. Check that the furniture fits together well – screwed or bolted, not glued.

Strong statements
ABOVE & OPPOSITE, TOP
Wooden furniture is particularly well suited to gardens with bold foliage planting, where its solid, no-nonsense form and colour seems to echo the natural outline of the plants. A bright orange canvas umbrella, above, picks up the colour of the terracotta tiles.

Baroque bravado
RIGHT An ornate wrought-iron chair has been painted electric blue, harmonizing surprisingly well with the big hosta leaves alongside.

Antique elegance
OPPOSITE, LEFT A former World War I field chair has been renovated to become a garden lounger.

Exotic splendour
OPPOSITE, RIGHT This unusual design (by New Zealander Diana Firth) has been painted an exotic shade of mauve to fit in with the colour scheme employed for the pool area.

Metal furniture

In the right circumstances, metals of various kinds can look attractive. You occasionally see small secluded courtyards in France and Italy furnished with inexpensive metal tables, and simple slatted chairs, more often than not painted dark green, which look perfect with the evergreen foliage – such as ivies and large-leaved fatsias – and terracotta containers that are often the most prominent features in shady gardens.

Cane and rattan

On balconies and verandahs with some overhead protection you can use less heavy-duty furniture – cane and rattan look good in these situations but they are materials that deteriorate quickly if alternately soaked and then scorched. If you use them out-of-doors, put them under cover when it rains.

Soft furnishings

Umbrellas and awnings are invaluable in sunny gardens, and particularly if you have opted for white-painted furniture which can glare uncomfortably in bright sunlight. Natural canvas or bright cottons in plain colours or simple geometric pattens look much more attractive than any of the man-made fibres with their gaudy chemical dyes.

Remember, too, that umbrellas need to be solidly anchored. I remember that years ago, when I installed a canvas umbrella from Italy in the roof garden I designed for a certain theatrical impressario, it took off in a gust of wind and fell in the street below, landing on a passing truck!

Awnings can add colour and life to a garden, and at night they provide a bit of shelter and protection. They are also very useful for providing shelter for hot tubs (see page 186). Those that are operated electrically must be of the best quality if they are going to function efficiently.

Neutral colours, cream or black and white, tend to set off the plants better than very gaudy colours, which would dominate the design in a small garden.

Eating al fresco

Cramped conditions in most towns and cities make it imperative to use the garden for entertaining and relaxation. Eating al fresco can be a source of great pleasure, provided the space is properly organized.

Food for fun
RIGHT Barbecuing is an increasingly popular summertime pursuit, and you can either have a portable barbecue like the one shown, which is ideal for entertaining small numbers, or you can opt for a large outdoor grill.

ONE OF THE greatest pleasures in life is sitting in the garden drinking a glass of wine or eating a good meal. Everything tastes better out-of-doors, and there is nothing like relaxing on a balmy summer's evening, surveying your garden as the sun sinks over the yard arm. If you want to use a portion of your garden for al fresco meals, you are almost certainly going to want to have a barbecue, and, as with any form of cooking activity, you need to think carefully about how you organize the space and the kind of equipment you will use.

A lot depends on your lifestyle, and whether you want to entertain frequently, and cater for large numbers. The first point to consider for any al fresco eating area is proximity to the food supply. Try to ensure that you have easy and quick access to the kitchen, and that you will not have to juggle with hot plates down an uneven path, or up and down awkward steps. There should be plenty of room for chairs to be pulled back from the table.

Barbecues

If you enjoy cooking, as well as eating, out-of-doors there is now an interesting range of barbecues to choose from, ranging from the simplest Japanese firebox type (*hibachi*) to large and elaborate models on which you could cater for a dinner party of 20 or more. Not only do the styles vary greatly, so do the means of heating the barbecue, from traditional charcoal to electric- or gas-fired versions. Some metal barbecues rust quite easily, and you will need somewhere to store them in wet weather.

It is also possible to design and build your own barbecue. If you do so, you need to consider first how many you will be catering for and what additional work space you might need. It is probably worthwhile taking this option if you barbecue a lot. You can then design and build a model with its own chimney, which will solve the problem of smoke and fumes irritating the diners. I have seen some attractive simple brick-built barbecues, with storage and work space built in. They are best sited in an unobtrusive corner, away from the dining area.

Whatever type of barbecue you opt for, you do need a worksurface nearby so that you can rest

179

tools and utensils, and plates, while you are barbe-cuing, although some models have built-in folding work trays and utensil holders, and often some storage areas as well. Heavier portable barbecues usually have wheels so that they can be moved around fairly easily; the smaller ones come as table top models, or have their own leg attachments. For the gas-operated or charcoal-based barbecues, you will need somewhere safe to store the fuel.

Siting the barbecuing area is an important factor, since neither the cook nor the guests want to be enveloped in a pall of smoke. Work out where your prevailing winds come from, and make sure that the barbecue area is downwind of the eating area.

Atmosphere and mood

The most enjoyable aspect of al fresco meals is their impromptu element, taking advantage of good weather or warm evenings. Lighting comes into its own here, enabling you to eat out at night, which is not only romantic but also great fun. Try to ensure that the lighting scheme is organized so that you have adequate light in the eating area, with exciting pools of light and dark in the areas beyond (see Lighting, pages 168-73).

Some form of protection and screening is useful for eating areas, as you are likely to feel any cold more intensely if sitting still in the evening. Large plants in containers make an excellent screen, and can be moved about, if needed, to protect diners from the wind, while awnings and umbrellas are vital for really hot, sunny days.

Bon appetit!
ABOVE & OPPOSITE The fun of eating out-of-doors is greatly enhanced by interesting table arrangements. You can collect leaves from the garden, and combine them with fruit and flowers, bring china and ornaments out of the house, to create a succulent still-life which looks inviting and entertaining.

Sculpture and ornament

Composed picture
BELOW, RIGHT An oriental
wood carving of sleeping
mother and child has
been turned into a small
composition in its own
right, in this tropical
garden. Wood carvings
are interesting subjects
to use, as their organic
appearance blends well
with the planting.

Decorative ceramics
BELOW Hand-made pots
are worthy subjects for
garden ornaments, as
this painted ceramic pot
by Linda Roberts
demonstrates. Large,
well-designed pots are
best left unplanted.

An attractive ornament or a well-proportioned piece of sculpture can make all the difference to a small garden, provided it is sited for maximum impact. Proportion, material and size are the key factors to consider when planning an ornamental feature of this sort.

SINCE MEDIEVAL TIMES, gardens have been decorated with a variety of different ornamental features – fountain heads, heraldic beasts, sundials, figures, urns and vases.

There is a great wealth of choice today of both traditional and modern ornaments, and some truly excellent modern sculpture and ceramics, but the most difficult job is probably to find the appropriate piece for the setting or, equally, to find the right setting for a given ornament.

Simply because the garden is small does not mean that the sculpture or ornament has to be scaled down in size to match, but the positioning does require special care. The aim is set off the ornament to greatest effect, so that it makes a very positive statement in the whole design. For this purpose the background, ideally, should be kept relatively simple – a plain wall, an expanse of paving, or, as far as plants are concerned, dark-leaved evergreens or large-leaved foliage plants. This simplicity will help to focus attention on the ornament. Lighting can be used to great effect at night in a small garden, with spotlights playing on a bust, for example, in a niche in a wall.

Anyone looking, for example, at the classical Italian gardens will see, immediately, how well the ornaments and sculpture fit into the architectural nature of the design. One of the secrets is to ensure that the materials used for the sculpture and ornaments blend well with those used for the paving, walls, and paths of the garden, both in texture and colour. Another is to ensure that the eye is led

Slate spires

LEFT Large pieces of sculpture, like these spires by Herta Keller, need to be positioned carefully. Here, their vertical geometric lines are nicely balanced by the plain rectangle of grass, with its equally strong geometric form.

Solid stone

ABOVE A handsome stone pedestal, left unadorned, can make a striking feature, or it can be used to provide a plinth for another display.

towards the sculpture by the features of the garden, by siting a container, perhaps, at the end of a vista or positioning a large pot to form a connecting link where paved and gravel surfaces meet.

Figures and animals

The popularity of figures in the garden dates back to Renaissance times, when statues were carved by the leading sculptors of the period. By the 17th century, figures were in demand in many of the great classical gardens in Britain, popular subjects being shepherds, cherubs and classical figures in stone, bronze or lead.

In oriental gardens, small replicas of Buddha are very popular, usually in stone, and fit well with the design. A number of interesting figures, in stone, bronze and wood, are now being imported from the Far East, which are ideally suited to the predominantly foliage gardens featured in this book.

Today, there is a wide range of reproductions of classical pieces of statuary to be found, but a more exciting alternative is to hunt around for a good modern piece by one of the growing band of young sculptors. These can often be found in sculpture gardens, like that run by my wife, Hannah Peschar. The advantage of viewing sculpture in a garden setting is obvious – you get a clear idea straightaway of the scale and setting required for the piece, and the opportunity to see how well it might fit with the features of your own garden.

Some of the best modern pieces of garden sculpture to opt for are those based on animals and birds, since these fit so well into the surrounding environment. Proportion and texture play an important part in the appropriate choice, and, again, choosing an appropriate setting is crucial to the overall impact.

Pots, urns and vases

Decorative terracotta containers have a long and honourable tradition in garden design, first found in Renaissance gardens in Italy and popular more or less ever since. There are so many styles to choose from – from elaborate, ornate and highly decorated urns with swags and garlands of flowers to wonderfully simple sculptural pots, like those created by Monica Young – that it would be hard not to find something to suit almost every type of design.

Any pot must have been fired properly so that it is frost-resistant, but the choice of style is one of personal taste. I like to see large pots used, unplanted, as a central feature in a garden.

Tanks and cisterns can make good ornaments in small gardens, particularly when positioned against a wall, perhaps with a spout or tap splashing water into it. If you can get hold of one, the lead cisterns used a couple of hundred years ago to collect rainwater are ideal, but not cheap. Reproductions can often be found, also in lead, which look just as good.

Getting ahead

OPPOSITE & BELOW LEFT These ceramic heads by sculptor Pat Volk need careful positioning to encourage a sense of mystery and excitement. In the picture opposite the head is surrounded by my favourite plant, *Petasites japonicus*. By contrast, the terracotta head (below left) is given a more prominent position in which foliage fades into the distance.

Mobile still-life

BELOW One of the advantages of small pieces of sculpture is that they can be moved about to create different moods.

185

Swimming pools and hot tubs

There is nothing to prevent you having a pool or a hot tub in a small garden, but it will need to be carefully planned. Plunge pools and hot tubs offer you the chance to relax without taking up valuable space.

Dipping in

RIGHT A timber hot tub is the best pool substitute for small spaces. Although you cannot swim in it, it is a very refreshing way of relaxing. This tub is 2m (6ft) in diameter and 1.2m (4ft) deep. It is surrounded by timber decking, and the tub itself is heated via the house boiler, with a pool filter to keep the water clean.

Splash of colour

BELOW This splash pool, which is about 4 by 3m (13 by 10ft), is ideal for any small suburban garden. Colourful planting around its edges makes using the pool more inviting. A small pool of this type is easy to maintain and reasonably inexpensive to heat.

IT NEVER FAILS to amaze me how rarely a swimming pool actually blends into the design of a small garden. Pool manufacturers who are not garden designers seem to have no feel for where a pool should be placed and how it should be fitted into the garden. When briefed by a client to include a swimming pool I treat it like any other water feature. It is an important part of the garden itself and should not look like an afterthought, even if it is.

Pools don't really need as much hard landscaping around them as most people tend to design. It is, of course, nice to have a place to sit at the pool's edge, but it is also attractive to bring plants and features right to the edge of the pool to improve the blending process. To assimilate a swimming pool into a small garden can be very difficult and in many cases a plunge pool with jets might be a better option. The water jets can be used to swim or lie against to create turbulence in the pool for extra fun. It is not as expensive to heat as a small pool and you may get more benefit from this type of swimming pool than from a large pool which, because of cost, is only heated for two to three months of the year.

Swimming pools come in all shapes and sizes – the choice depends on the way in which it can be incorporated easily into the garden. In a small garden where a swimming pool may be taking up most of the available space, an informal lagoon style pool may be the best shape to go for. Don't go for exaggerated curves; an irregular shape with perhaps a backdrop of rocks and plants contained by a retaining wall would be a better way of blending your pool into your garden. Rectangular shapes very often look best if sited asymmetrically.

Safety and maintenance

There are unfortunately quite a few practical and safety elements that have to be taken into design when installing a pool. First and foremost, be careful not to use any material that can be slippery when wet as decking or paving around the pool. Stones or tiles should be regularly cleaned after the winter to clean off any algae or slippery material that has formed over the winter months. Composite fine aggregate materials are very often used as edging to pools to prevent just this happening. Small pools are easy to cover and this is a very important factor for safety for very small children. The cover should be tightly fastened around the edges and safe enough for a child or adult to stand on it without it giving way. It must be easily attached with minimum fuss and bother after the pool has been used. These covers can be combined with heat insulation ones to keep the pool warm after heating.

In many countries it is a legal requirement to have a proper fence around your pool to a standard specification. This, in a small garden, would be very difficult to achieve but can be done by trellis or using the external walls of the garden as a security measure. If you have small children then it is very necessary to consider all aspects of safety and have

Mosaic pattern

RIGHT & ABOVE The edge of this pool in Diana Firth's garden has been very cleverly designed by her with a mosaic-type tiling pattern surrounding it. The pool itself, below, is like a large spa pool (about 3m by 2.5m/10ft by 8ft) with swimming jets. Sinking the swimming pool below ground level, as this one has been, has given extra privacy and protection from the sea winds.

a lockable door or gate which divides the pool from the rest of the garden so that children cannot in any way get through into the pool area.

Pool surrounds

Decking, if I dare mention it again, is sometimes the perfect solution for the edge of a small plunge pool. Its flexibility allows it to be constructed in such a way that it can provide sun-bathing areas which may slightly overhang the pool or break up sharp corners of a square or rectangular shape.

Good plants to use around swimming pools are those which are evergreen but give an interesting

shape all year round such as palms, *Trachycarpus fortunei*, *Chamerops humilis* or *Phoenix* in pots for the summer or maybe cordylines, phormiums or yuccas. However avoid very spiny plants as you do not wish to get hurt by them.

Hot tubs

Hot tubs were invented in California as a means of having an invigorating bath in the garden. Old wine vats were converted into tubs full of hot water, rather like a Japanese bath, in which the body is massaged by high-powered jets of hot water. They are usually made from hardy redwoods, cedar or Douglas fir, and can also be made from any similar timber that is resistant to moisture.

Most tubs are from 1.5m to 2.5m (5ft to 8ft) in diameter. A 2.5m (8ft) hot tub, which can hold up to eight people, is great fun at barbecues and garden parties. In many ways hot tubs are preferable to swimming pools because they are usually less work, fit more easily into a small space and can be turned off and on for winter and summer with minimum fuss. The hot tub has seats inside which brings the hot water comfortably up to chin level. The circulation of the water is important to keep it clean and so there are pumps, filters and heaters employed and the water is either blown or bubbled through jets in the side of the tub.

Tubs can be sited just next to the house or in a position where you can walk comfortably from the house over a deck or hard surface to get into them with minimum fuss. I have seen hot tubs placed on roof gardens or even on elevated verandahs. Screening the hot tub – both for privacy and shelter – is important. You can use very lush groups of bamboos or large palms in pots or even design a pergola over the top which can give you added privacy from neighbours.

The same physical requirements are needed as for a swimming pool – a supply of water and electricity and somewhere to put the filter and the heating system. Again, timber decking is an obvious choice for the surrounds for hot tubs and spas, and looks particularly good, especially with a tub where it can be built at different levels and adapted to include extra seating space, storage and planting spaces.

Beach effect
LEFT Large pebbles and a curving edge to the pool help to create a coastal appearance in this garden. Big-leaved plants, butting up to the pool edge, give shelter and soften the surrounds.

Conservatories

A conservatory offers the opportunity to grow wonderfully exotic plants with large rich flowers and immense jungle-like foliage, and, if well designed, can make a useful link between house and garden.

CONSERVATORIES, or garden rooms, have been with us since Victorian times, when the plant hunters started to bring back exotic tropical plants that could thrive only in sheltered conditions, and with lots of light. After a long period in the doldrums, the conservatory is once again popular, with an increasing number of specialist companies offering a wide range of designs.

Style

Ideally the conservatory should link the house to the garden, its architectural form in sympathy with that of the house. One of the most attractive, and useful, options in town houses with limited space is to use the narrow alley which runs down the back extension of the house for a conservatory. As with all additions to your house, you will have to seek the appropriate planning permission, and observe building regulations.

The main points to attend to in choosing the style and size of the conservatory, apart from any financial consideration, are firstly what and how you will use the conservatory – is it primarily for the plants or primarily as an additional room; are the floors suitably constructed; is the conservatory adequately insulated, ventilated and shaded? Then you can start thinking about the design considerations.

The link between the conservatory and the garden should not be overlooked. You could, for example, ensure that the colour of the painted surfaces on the conservatory is picked up on a seat, gate or small building in the garden. Ensure that some plants are grown close to the conservatory to blend the planting within with that without.

Elements of planning

Conservatories are a great asset in a temperate climate, as they increase the range of plants that we

Green link
RIGHT This conservatory acts as a link between the kitchen and the garden, extending the garden path through to the house, with rich, dense planting of climbers and ferns. Citrus fruit is grown in pots on either side. The floor tiles are imported African slate, which come in a good range of subtle colours.

Cool and shaded
OPPOSITE This north-facing lean-to conservatory has a grape vine running across the roof. A built-in border down one side houses evergreen plants, and flower colour comes from pelargoniums in pots, and various tender or half-hardy plants, including streptocarpus and lilies.

Living with plants
RIGHT A conservatory like
this one is very much a
garden room. Plants are
arranged around the
sitting spaces and soft
furnishings make it both
relaxed and welcoming.
In small spaces like
conservatories, it pays to
use a limited colour
palette for the planting in
order to unify the design
and emphasize it.

can grow, and for the owner of a small garden, it is
well worth considering turning a small part of the
plot over to a conservatory, where you can over-
winter more interesting plants that you then put out
in pots in the summer months. Exotic plants have
many of the virtues I admire most – wonderful
forms and handsome large leaves, with the bonus,
sometimes, of truly stunning flowers and delicious,
heady scent.

Two factors will determine which types of plant
you can grow in the conservatory – one is whether
the conservatory is heated night and day in winter,
and the other is the aspect – the direction the conservatory faces. South-facing conservatories can become
extremely hot in summer, and adequate forms of
ventilation and shading, in the form of blinds, may be
necessary, both for the plants, and for you, to be
comfortable in it.

Roller blinds fixed to the inside of the glazing, or cedar shutters on the outside, are obvious choices, but there is a wide range to choose from.

Plants will not thrive unless the conservatory is well-ventilated. Air should be circulated from the bottom to the top of the conservatory, and you may need to include an electric fan or vent.

Plants for the conservatory

The containers used for the plants must be good quality, and they must be planned as an ensemble. Do not dot the plants about, particularly if there are only a few; group them in one eye-catching arrangement. If possible, ensure that the plants furnish several levels of the conservatory, so incorporate climbers, tall shrubs or ferns, and make sure there is adequate shelf or table space for smaller plants.

Plants which are useful for dry and arid conservatories are the cacti and succulents that flourish naturally in these conditions. They do not have to be spiky little objects in small pots. Opt instead for big aloes or agaves, echiverias or echinocacti, or *Aeonium arboreum*, which are all generous-sized plants which do well in pots. Yuccas and some palms will take dry conditions, but they do need a reasonable amount of light.

Conservatories offer a great benefit in allowing you to eat more or less 'al fresco' all the year round, and the joy of having scented plants around you, or 'exotic' looking flowers, such as mandevilla or jasmine, in spring, when nothing else is in flower in the garden.

One of the other great joys in the conservatory is to grow tropical water plants in large pots of water. *Thalia*, *Lotus* and *Zantedeschia* can all be grown successfully in the conservatory, but they do need plenty of sun to flourish, and the water will have to be topped up frequently.

One of the most successful systems for containing plants in the conservatory is to create a permanent bed, rather than simply using containers. This will allow you to grow larger plants, such as trees and vigorous climbers, as the root run will be less restricted, although the disadvantage is that you will not be able to move the plants about. A simple raised bed running along one wall can also incorporate a sitting area, or some cupboards as well. It is important in the conservatory to incorporate adequate storage space so that any messy gardening equipment is out of sight when not in use.

Try to ensure that the furniture suits the style of the conservatory, and avoid too much clutter, if possible. A few large plants are a much better choice than a myriad small ones, and a couple of good climbing plants helps to give the conservatory a more exotic feel, as do baskets or pots with trailing plants fixed on brackets at higher levels – either to the walls or the ceiling.

Managing the environment

It is vital that the plants are in good condition; far better to have a few, really well kept, lush and healthy plants than any number with browning or sparse foliage. In heated indoor rooms, many plants suffer more from lack of humidity in the air than lack of water; ferns are notoriously susceptible to dry air. Shading is crucial in most conservatories, particularly south- or west-facing ones, in summer.

Summer houses and gazebos

Although associated more often with larger gardens, a summerhouse or gazebo, tucked into a corner of a small garden, creates a delightful sense of seclusion and privacy, especially if covered in climbing plants

A SUMMER HOUSE or gazebo may seem an extravagance in a small garden, but it provides the same benefits that it does in a large garden: somewhere quiet and relaxed to sit, away from the bustle of the house. The size and degree of shelter afforded by the gazebo will depend on individual needs, but for most purposes the shelter is primarily overhead, with some kind of screening at the sides to give privacy and to keep the wind off. Wood and metal are the most commonly used materials, and can be highly finished or fairly rough and rustic, whichever you prefer.

A well-designed pergola can provide a useful visual link between house and garden, and at the same time afford much-needed shade for a sitting area in summer. Good proportions are crucial to the visual success of the pergola: structures should not look top-heavy or unnecessarily fragile. The materials are numerous: brick, stone, metal and wood can all look attractive in the right situation. Simple structures made from rough hewn wood can be built relatively easily and cheaply. The wood must first be treated with preservative, otherwise it will rot.

Hideaway
LEFT A modern pavilion built right across the bottom of this tiny Sydney garden not only provides shelter from the weather, but is an ideal place to escape for solitude and relaxation.

Cool retreat
BELOW A circular gazebo, supported on pillars, thatched with reed and half-hidden under a canopy of creeper, makes a hideaway at the end of this white garden in which *Cosmos* and 'Iceberg' roses contrast with clipped evergreens.

195

Climbing plants

The quality of the planting is as important here as it is elsewhere in the garden. Most pergolas look best with a generous covering of large-leaved climbers. In a mixed collection of plants, aim to have at least a few with good scent, and try to ensure a succession of flowers.

Other good plants are *Aristolochia durior* (syn. *macrophylla*), the Dutchman's pipe, with its handsome heart-shaped large leaves, *Actinidia chinensis*, the kiwi fruit, of which you must plant both a male and female form if you want to produce fruit, and *Akebia quinàta*, which is excellent for shade. For sheltered, warm spots, grow the passion flower (*Passiflora caerulea*) or *Lonicera hildebrandiana*, the latter being deliciously scented.

Bowers, arches and arbours are all variations on the same theme, usually incorporating a seat. The structures can vary from the exotic to the stark, depending on the mood of the garden, and can stand as a feature in their own right, or simply provide a useful support for a range of climbing plants. Traditionally roses have been used in these situations and those with good green foliage and wafts of scent are 'Albertine', with its double pink flowers in June, the vigorous 'Paul's Himalayan Musk', which is also beautifully scented, *Rosa longicuspis* 'Wedding Day' and *R. filipes* 'Kiftsgate' with its clouds of white flowers.

Classical designs for arches can also be successfully incorporated into small garden designs, but any tall structure needs to be carefully positioned so that it does not stand out in a sea of small plants.

Gilded cage

RIGHT This ornate Thai summer house sits above an inky pool where bird cages and tropical plants provide additional interest. The idea could work as well in cooler climates with a similar timber structure set over either a pond or a planting scheme of ferns and bamboos.

Chinese pavilion

OPPOSITE Designed by Sue Farrell, this little pavilion is beautifully framed by the planting, its warm gold colour adding to the feeling of comfort.

Fantasy and fun

Where growing space is at a premium, it often pays to opt for fantasy instead, using imaginative ideas to overcome the problems of the site, painting in flowers on a wall where, for example, none will grow or expanding the boundaries of a garden with a trompe l'oeil of a view through a painted doorway.

SINCE THE ROMANTIC period of garden history, which started in the late 18th century, a few garden designers have been determined to use their gardens as settings for their wildest fantasies. In Victorian times, there was a great penchant for extraordinary follies, grottos and other flights of fancy, eminently suited to some of the large country house gardens of the times. However, even in a small garden, there is nothing to prevent you letting your imagination rip, although the limitations of scale make it more difficult to achieve the element of surprise that is usually a basic requirement for the execution of any fantasy idea.

One of the most successful ways of approaching fantasy in the garden is to think of the garden as a stage set, and to use the boundaries as one would the backdrop to a stage. If you wish to expand the actual boundaries of a small garden why not create a *trompe l'oeil* – in other words, deceive the eye – by painting in false features? For example, in the end wall of a small town garden, a fake doorway can be created, with the door left apparently ajar to reveal a tantalizing glimpse of an illusory garden beyond.

Paint effects

In areas of the garden where light is at a premium, such as in basements, the walls can be painted white and artificial flowers then painted in. The only limitations are your ability to conceive the ideas, and then execute them. If you are going to do the work yourself, then it is important to select ideas that you can carry out well enough to achieve a professional-looking finish.

Using cheap modern materials to create classical-looking antiques is another form of visual deceit that works well in gardens, where the onlooker is not necessarily close enough to detect the visual trick being played upon him or her. There are now some ready-mixed paint effects you can use to distress or age materials that work so well that even the experts have difficulty distinguishing the false from the real thing. Imitation verdigris – the greenish patina you get on old bronze or copper – is now easily created using a pre-mixed paint and is ideal for any metal ornaments or relics. Alternatively, a concrete pedestal could be painted in terracotta, and then colour washed to age it, and amazingly realistic marble effects can be painted on concrete pillars and columns if you want to go for a rococo Italianate style.

The Italianate atmosphere could be enhanced by distressing walls to give the appearance of the soft pinky brown colours of Tuscan villas, with small false windows painted in to its expanse.

Freehand painted effects are rather more challenging, and unless you are naturally artistic, it is probably better to opt for simpler geometrically based images. Painting in fake columns and pillars does not require great artistic imagination, and can lend a special touch to the garden as a backdrop, for example, to a small formal pool.

One of the most useful materials for creating illusory effects is trelliswork, which is light, easy to construct and very versatile. Screening parts of the

Through the looking glass
OPPOSITE Almost the entire wall of the house has been faced with a mirror, into which has been set an antique false window, giving a splendid reflection of the rest of the garden. The antique bath set in front, filled with water lettuce, came from India.

Everlasting flowers
BELOW A *trompe l'oeil* painting glows from a deceptive trellis frame, painted the colour of verdigris. This gives the illusion you can step into another world, cleverly led on by terracotta pots of *Clivia miniata*.

199

Spiritual welcome
BELOW Wrapping the trunk of a tree in multi-coloured silks is an ancient Buddhist practice to celebrate the spirit of an old tree in which elephant effigies are offered as gifts in return for granted wishes.

Doing bird
BELOW RIGHT This is not a penthouse for London's sparrows, but a futuristic bird house by Diana Firth.

Tongue-in-cheek
OPPOSITE This fantasy feature by garden designer Tony Noel adds humour, with style, to his London town garden.

garden with trellis helps trick the eye into thinking that the garden is, perhaps, wider and squarer than it really is. Mirrors can be incorporated into trellis arches, for example, to reflect back a particular feature. Water is singularly successfully reflected in this way, and will enlarge an otherwise tiny garden.

The real size of a water feature can be disguised by using decking to cover the edges, so that the water apparently disappears underneath it, creating an artificial bridge.

It is important to work out how to combine any fantasy effects with the rest of the garden. A small path leading up to a *trompe l'oeil* door is essential if the visual deceit is going to work. Alternatively one part of the garden can be used for one of the wilder flights of fancy – a small area at the end of the garden, perhaps, being turned into an 18th-century grotto, complete with deep pool, mask-head fountain and imitation rocks, planted with mossy plants, ferns, and ivies, perhaps.

Old paintings are full of wonderful tricks of perspective, and if you are looking for ideas to copy for a *trompe l'oeil* feature for your garden, you may well find just the inspiration you are looking for in these. A boring expanse of wall can be enlivened by creating a false alcove, in which a bust or staute can be placed, giving depth and focus to the garden.

Another interesting idea is to take some local feature, and elaborate upon it in your garden. One London garden has mimicked the features of the canal it backs onto in its own garden, duplicating the bridge and water feature within its own boundaries. Or a part of the garden could be turned over to resemble an area of ancient ruins, with bits of broken porticos, columns and urns lying, apparently abandoned, in a small shady area of the garden, half hidden by creepers.

Sadly to say, we seem to have lost our forefathers' penchant for the absurd or unusual, and maybe now is the time to reawaken that sense of fun. Perhaps a large chessboard with huge chess pieces could be incorporated into a patio, or an ornamental bird-cage, complete with stuffed birds, could be hung from a tree. One of the greatest elements of fantasy gardening is water, and many years ago I designed a water canal that had mirrors at each end where it reached the boundary walls of the garden. It gave the illusion that the water continued for many miles either side, as if it were running through an archway in the wall.

Visual jokes and illusions
On the whole, fantasy effects are best used in moderation if the aim is genuinely to deceive the eye. Some gardeners have taken fantasy effects as a theme and created a whole series of optical illusions

and visual jokes, but for most people the most successful use of fantasy effects is to turn the physical limitations of the site to advantage, where a dark alleyway becomes a mysterious grotto, for example.

Great care needs to be taken with humorous fantasy effects because the joke can quickly pall. These ideas are best restricted to less frequently used parts of the garden rather than an area which is constantly in view.

One of my favourite gardens in Holland, however, was a small town garden where the owner had planted up a whole series of bizarre containers – pianos, lavatories, cisterns, top hats and so forth – which formed a theme in the garden. Ivan Hicks, the British garden designer, has also very successfully

included a whole range of wacky pieces of sculpture with some well chosen plants to set them off.

Roof gardens, being dissociated from any other planting, are one of the best places to try out unusual, fantasy ideas. One look at the roof garden on the former Derry and Toms building in London, with its Egyptian temples, Alhambra-style water gardens and flamingoes, is proof. The high-level setting of a roof garden lends itself to the creation of a Moorish garden for example, with cut-out trelllis providing a suitably ornate backdrop, exotic tiling for the floor and carefully chosen Mediterranean-style plants.

Lighting plays an important part in creating illusions of depth and space, and in dramatizing the effects you are trying to achieve.

Esoteric collection
RIGHT & OPPOSITE Fantasy does not come much whackier than this in these theatrical set pieces by Ivan Hicks. Salvage yards are an ideal hunting ground for material for just such a collection of *objets trouvés*.

Index

Acknowledgments

Garden designers

Anthony Paul* (Ockley, Surrey, UK), 14-27, 32-5, 39, 50, 55, 56-7, 77, 80-81, 88-89, 91-4, 95T, 96T, 97, 101, 106-7, 110, 112, 113C, 114-5, 117T, 132, 134-5, 141, 153T, 155R, 156B, 159B and T, 160, 161T and R, 162B, 164, 165BL/BR, 171, 178-9, 181R, 186, 187R, 189, 199

Rod Barnett* (Auckland, NZ) 40-41, 46, 112TL, 121B, 122B

John Brookes* (Fontwell, Sussex, UK) 120B, 124T, 148L

Beth Chatto* (Colchester, Essex, UK) 165T

The Chelsea Gardener* (London, UK) 58, 128B

Marshall Cook 61

Trevor Crump* (Sydney, Aus) 194

Sue Farrell 73, 96B, 137, 166-7, 190, 197

Christine Ferneyhough* (Auckland, NZ) 62B, 63, 76, 78, 127, 140T, 149, 174, 175B

Diana Firth* (Auckland, NZ) 86L, 86-7C, 177BR, 188T, 188-9L, 200R

Sue Firth* (Auckland, NZ) 54, 59, 160B, 176-7T

Good Manors Landscaping* (Sydney, Aus) 53, 11B

Hailstone Landscaping* (Adelaide, Aus) 47B, 119L

Pam Hailstone* (Adelaide, Aus) 79

Ivan Hicks*/Gardens in Mind (Rowlands Castle, Hants, UK) 138/9L, 161BL, 202, 203

Martin Lane Fox 136, 143B, 192-3

Christopher Lloyd (Great Dixter, UK) 142

Lord Alistair McAlpine 102, 195

Eiji Morozumi* (Perth, Aus) 6B, 64-5, 100, 129T

Tony Noel* (London, UK) 48, 68, 70-71, 118, 138T, 158, 176B, 201

Walda Pairon* (Antwerp, Belgium) 2-3, 6T, 8-9, 28-31, 66-7, 150-51L, 177T

Nori and Sandra Pope (Hadspen House, Somerset, UK) 151B

Robert Railley* (Auckland, NZ) 38, 109

Richard and Jenny Raworth (UK) 191

Mien Ruys Gardens* (Dedemsvaart, Holland) 130-31, 154, 155L, 160L

David Scott* (UK) 11

Ted Smyth* (Auckland, NZ) 99, 169R, 172-3

Martin Summers 7

Bill Warren* (Bangkok, Thailand) 60, 98, 103, 105, 125T, 170, 196

Henk Weijers* (Haarlem, Holland) 12-13, 74-5, 90, 116, 117B, 152R, 163BR

Annie Wilkes and Richard Haigh* (Sydney, Aus) 10B, 10T, 36-7, 43, 47T, 51B, 52, 69, 125B, 126, 153B, 168, 183R, 198

* Professional garden designers.
B=below, C=centre, L=left, R=right, T=top

Anthony Paul and Steven Wooster would like to thank the following for kind permission to photograph their gardens:

Peter Aldington (UK)
Monica Amstad (Switzerland)
Stuart and Christine Averill (UK)
Mr and Mrs Leo Blik (UK)
Mr and Mrs Bob Bridges (UK)
Ruth Brittain and family (NZ)
Mrs Coode-Adams (Feeringbury Manor, UK)
Mrs Phil Cooke and family (NZ)
Paul Fearmen (Aus)
Mr and Mrs Charles Fenwick (UK)
Val Flavell (NZ)
Jenny Gibbs (NZ)
Val Hackel (Switzerland)
Jonathan and Madeleine Hilton (UK)
Himeji Japanese Garden (Aus)
Mrs de Jong (Holland)
Gilly Knight (UK)
Max and Axelle Koch (Switzerland)
Paul and Denise Lincoln-Smith (Aus)
Mr and Mrs Lynn (Aus)
Liz and Jonathan Mansfield (UK)
Roger and Jack Mavity (UK)
Shirley Nicholson (UK)
Richard and Sharon Noble (UK)
Mrs O'Hay (UK)
Michael Paul (UK)
Sue of Takapuna (NZ)
Baron and Baroness Sweerts de Landas Wyborgh (UK)
Turtle House, Bangkok (Thailand)
Marisa Vivavnidya (Thailand)
Mr and Mrs Weerman (Holland)
Mr and Mrs Peter Wilson (UK)
Mark Woloshyn (UK)

Special thanks for their kindness and hospitality to: Mark Barnett and family (Aus); Chris and Karen Collins (Aus); Mark Hampson-Tindale (Aus); Gil Hanly (NZ); Andy and Heather MacIntosh (NZ); Bill Warren (Thailand).

Author's acknowledgments

I would like to offer special thanks to the following: Steven Wooster for his artistry in design and photography; Susan Berry for her general guidance; Polly Powell and Barbara Dixon at HarperCollins for their faith and enthusiasm; Mike Paul for his help with styling for the photographs on pages 178-9, Andy Butcher for his help in drawing garden plans and last, but not least, to Hannah, Custard and Beaver, for their company and love.

Some of the sculptors' and ceramicists' work in this book can be seen at the Hannah Peschar Sculpture Garden, Ockley, Surrey (tel: 0306 627 269; fax: 0306 627 662).